D0189013

Whose Stuff Is This?

Praise for *Whose Stuff Is This?*

A comprehensive book for anyone interested in developing their intuition and psychic abilities. Presented in an easy-to-read manner, Yvonne has created an encyclopedia of knowledge pertaining to the healing arts. What a joy and a blessing! I look forward to recommending this wonderful book.
~ Harriette Knight, author of *CHAKRA POWER! How to Fire Up Your Energy Centers to Live a Fuller Life*

Realizing you're an empath immediately brings up a million questions. This book is an extensive library of answers that can help you figure out what's going on while also empowering you to do something about it!
~ Elise Lebeau, M.Sc., Professional Intuitive, Founder of the EmpathCommunity.EliseLebeau.com

Simply put, this book should be required reading for all human beings as we continue to learn how to navigate our energy bodies while being in a physical body. With thorough research and case examples, this book provides everything you need to know from identifying when you are picking up on others' energy to practical tips on what to do about it. The information on setting boundaries is really a must-read for everyone whether you consider yourself to be an empath or not.   ~ Tisha Morris, author of *27 Things to Feng Shui Your Home*

Anyone who has experienced unexplained mood, energy, or emotional changes, can benefit from the information in this book. So many people are unaware of the effect others have on their moods or health. In an instant happy turns to sad or mad. Over time this can cause disease. Learning to detach and screen out any harmful negative emotions of others is necessary for good health and relationships. This helps us remain compassionate and effective in all areas of our life and in all of our many roles as person, healer, friend, mother, or coworker.   ~ Denise DeMaras, artist and holistic spiritual health counselor certified by Chopra University

Yvonne Perry provides a brilliant, much-needed guidebook for children and adults whose gift of empathy can also be their greatest challenge. She presents stories that offer strategies for one's emotional overwhelm and spiritual expression. The excellent techniques to use this gift of emotional connection in alignment with one's soul's purpose give all hope. ~ Devra Ann Jacobs, president, Dancing Word Group LLC

Yvonne Perry's book, *Whose Stuff Is This?* thoroughly explains the process of being an empath in today's world. She provides cognitive, emotional, physical, energetic, and spiritual explanations for the origin of deep empathy, while sharing her own amazing story and the stories of others. This book offers an array of powerful techniques to help empathic people create healthy boundaries, stay balanced, and release other people's energy and emotions from their personal space. This book is a must read for anyone and everyone who is sensitive to the thoughts, moods and problems of those around them.   ~ Gini Grey, transformational coach and author of the book, *From Chaos to Calm: How to Shift Unhealthy Stress Patterns and Create Your Own Balance in Life*.

Each of us is affected by the energy and emotions around us. We often assume that what we are feeling "Is Us" and not a byproduct of our ability to sense the world around us. *Whose Stuff Is This?* can support each of us as we learn to identify who "We Are" and separate ourselves from the din. It is a must read for the emotionally sensitive or those wanting to develop this intuitive gift.   ~ Rita Louise, PhD, founder of the Institute of Applied Energetics and author of *Avoiding the Cosmic 2x4* soulhealer.com

This high-level guidebook, *Whose Stuff Is This?* takes the reader on an inner voyage to reconnect within, to review emotional connectivity to others, and to avoid psychic overload. Empathic persons can easily be drained or over-stimulated. Newly awakening empathy is best cultivated with understanding of the empathic capabilities and author Yvonne Perry shows you how to proceed most advantageously. ~ Tom Goode ND, DD

Yvonne's work is beautiful, well written, and personable. It speaks directly to the heart and makes it okay to be exactly who you are. It is educational and comforting to read, yet not about filling your head with book knowledge—instead, filling the holes of unexplained experiences with a feeling of empowerment and compassion for self and others as we face the pain and trauma on this journey toward wholeness. ~ Reverend Cherise Thorne, founder of New Dawn Ascension http://www.knowingspirit.org

Yvonne Perry's intelligent book expresses the challenges that come along with the gifts of being an empath or sensitive. Her expressive stories are a natural way to relate and communicate the effect that being sensitive has on us. Her approach is by far a very easy way to understand not only how we can deal with others but a way to connect to them. It is a much-needed book that explains why there are benefits to aligning and attracting positive energy and why detaching from negative personalities is so vital to our holistic health and well-being. After all, we want to know the answer to "Whose Stuff Is This?" so that we can apply the necessary solutions. ~ Anna Maria Prezio, Ph.D., Bestselling author of *Confessions of a Feng Shui Ghost-Buster*, holistic spiritual health practitioner, Feng Shui Master, CEO of Feng Shui Harmony.

Whose Stuff Is This?

Finding Freedom from the Thoughts, Feelings, and Energy of Those Around You

Yvonne Perry

Write On! Publishing
Nashville, Tennessee

Copyright © 2010 by Yvonne Perry

Whose Stuff Is This? Finding Freedom from the Thoughts, Feelings, and Energy of Those Around You

Published and printed in the United States of America.

All rights reserved. Under International Copyright Law, no part of this book may be reproduced, stored, or transmitted by any means–electronic, mechanical, photographic (photocopy), recording, or otherwise–without the written permission from the publisher.

Cover art by Hayley John. Cover design by Rick Chappell.

Trade Paper ISBN: 978-0-9825722-4-5
E-Book ISBN: 978-0-9825722-5-2
Write On! Publishing
February 2011

http://tinyurl.com/whosestuff

Disclaimer: This book contains the opinions and thoughts of its authors and is not intended to provide professional services or medical advice. The publisher/authors claims no responsibility or liability for loss or risk incurred as a result of the use or application of any of the contents of the book. Some of the characteristics that empaths display can also be diagnosed as ADD, agoraphobia, bipolar disorder, or clinical depression. This book is not intended for making diagnoses or treatment of any illness. Contact your healthcare professional if you need help with a mental health issue.

Contents

Acknowledgements

Thank you to those who helped proofread this book: Sally Hinkle, Denise Demaras, Randall Hawk, and Dana Micheli.

Gratitude to those who contributed stories or allowed me to write about their experiences: Hillary Raimo, Tom Goode, Zeb McCurley, Amanda McCurley, Sandy, Samantha, Bridgette, Iris Erielle Feliciano Foss, Gloria Mitchell, Gini Grey, and Caron Goode.

Much appreciation to those who gave endorsements: Denise Demaras, Elise Lebeau, Gini Grey, Barbara Techel, Tisha Morris, Harriette Knight, Rita Louise, PhD, Sondra Ray, Devra Ann Jacobs, Gini Grey, Tom Goode, Luis Angel Diaz, Lynn Serafinn, Anna Maria Prezio, and Elizabeth Diamond.

Thank you, Universe, for the experiences I have had that allow me to share this healing heart message to empaths everywhere.

Dedication

To all empaths everywhere—especially those who have unknowingly been adversely affected by the energy of others.

Foreword

Our greatest gift can become our greatest challenge.

Our challenge in the 21st century is to cultivate high touch in tandem to the continuing evolution of high-tech. As our computers, smart phones and yet-to-be-manifested new ideas become the items with which we bond, the biological need to connect still resides within us and will not go away. Humans are literally hardwired for connection with each other.

Neuroscience has demonstrated the connection pathways. A good example of this is the system of mirror neurons located throughout the brain. They help us read other people's feelings and actions, and these neurons may be the foundations of empathy. For example, two people in conversation stimulate each other's mirror neuron system. Whether the emotions beneath the words concern happiness, shame, sadness, or jubilance, similar facial muscles will move and the same areas of the brain turn on. We do resonate with each other, and specific people—whose central nervous systems are more sensitive than others—feel deeper and so resonate with others so much that they over-identify with emotional pain. Likewise, they move to alleviate suffering, to support or help quickly. We call these persons "empaths."

This wonderful book on the topic of empathy addresses the needs and care of the sensitive person—the one who easily identifies with another's emotional state and can genuinely understand another's intention to action and can also intuit appropriate care, words, or actions to alleviate the suffering of another. Empaths, by their very nature, are intuitive and even psychic.

Empathy is the ability to understand the internal experiences, that is, the feelings, thoughts, and intentions of another. An empath cannot turn off this trait, as they are born to be the empaths they are. Oxytocin is a hormone, sometimes called the love hormone, in mammals that is the bonding hormone in the female giving birth, breastfeeding, and connecting biochemically to her child. On a larger scale, this hormone promotes feelings of romantic love. New research indicates that people who are most empathic were found to have a variation of an oxytocin receptor gene.

The character trait of empathy, especially in women who seem more hard-wired than men to be empathic, can rule people's lives. Many enter into helping professions such as teaching, nursing, mental health, elder care, and parenthood; sine become a nanny or caregiver. Many of these empaths feel depressed, lose motivation, and develop stress disorders. Moreover, they do not recognize boundaries or emotional borders, despite their professional roles and personal stamina.

Empathy has been described as the glue that holds human connections together. But, what happens when those sensitive people get stuck in the glue, and their talent becomes their challenge, like having an illness to face each day? I've seen the condition repeatedly in clients with whom I've worked—those who lose themselves to their work; those who become entangled in others' problems; those who give away their heart and energy until depleted; those who change professions, choose to work alone, or choose not to go into public arenas. Why? They feel too much, and their circuits become overloaded. These situations are part of the bad news, but don't let it bring you down.

The best news is we live in a phenomenal period. The renaissance of empathy is happening right now. We are living it! Doctors are calling for the return of treating patients with empathy, not drugs. Philosophers like Jeremy Rifkin, author of *The Empathic Civilization*, discuss the new times we enter, after cycles of consumption and greed, as guided by empathy. Rifkin asks if humanity can reach a collective empathy in time to avoid further disaster. Perhaps this virtue of empathy, a recognized worldly virtue, can empower empathic people to learn to care for their souls as humankind learns to care for the planet and for each other. The time for this book is right now because the time for empaths to teach others about connection and resonance in positive ways is here.

Mother Theresa said, "We can do no great things—only small things with great love." So empaths, in order to accomplish great things, let us begin with small acts of love for ourselves. In my experience as a spiritual counselor and coach, sensitive empaths usually began their empowerment journey to strength with a path of self-awareness. The path's journey has only one purpose, that you remain whole and centered, and not become drained, fractured, or out of kilter.

The benefit of reading the stories in this book prepared by Yvonne Perry is that you will recognize that you are not alone. Most empaths are silent sufferers. Yvonne has given voice and words to those stories.

Many empaths are members of communities and service organizations, and sometimes we get sucked into the roles that need to be played and the duties that need to be carried out. We can inhabit the role so thoroughly, we get lost. We are so dutiful in the tasks we volunteer for that we burn out. We are so enthusiastic, we can carry other people right along until one day we sag under the weight. We flood others with our love until we drown them. Yvonne Perry lived through several of these scenarios and knows firsthand the mental anxiety and emotional draining that happens to a bright, healthy, loving woman, wife, mom . . . and . . . and . . . and . . . Personal experience and professional training make this author the best to present truth as empaths feel it and know it, and to provide the steps to recovery and renewal.

I asked her to write this book for the men and women living with the empathic talents who are unable to fly because of the burden of empathy. She guides you skillfully in unburdening, flapping your wings, testing your flight, and then rising high on the resonant waves of connection with the strength to bring others up with you.

As empaths, we are a new tribe forming, finding each other, and gaining strength in knowing how to revitalize ourselves. Take heart in knowing that the empathy fatigue described by Yvonne is real, and many suffer with it unknowingly. How important it is for you to recognize your symptoms in these pages! How gratifying and healing for you to find strategies that work. We cannot change our natures, and we shouldn't suffer any longer because of our talent. Onward empaths, to showing yourself the same kindness you give others so that you may do great things for many.

~ Dr. Caron Goode, ED.D., NCC, DAPA, author of *The Art & Science of Coaching Parents, Raising Intuitive Children,* and *Kids Who See Ghosts - Guide Them Through Their Fears*

Introduction

The word "empath" may be a new term for some readers, but an ever-increasing number of people are reporting that they are sensitive to all types of energy, including those produced by other humans, the environment, electromagnetic frequencies, geophysical stress, and even non-physical beings. Being empathic simply means you are able to pick up on the energy of others—we can all do that to some degree—but some people are so sensitive to environmental stimuli and the emotional energy of others that it causes disturbances in their health and life. Empirical evidence suggest that some people seem to have unique variations in their central nervous system that cause them to have an unusual sensitivity to light, smell, sound, taste, and touch, and may be very intuitive. Some are so detrimentally affected that they rarely go into public because they feel overwhelmed by the energy they pick up. These highly-sensitive individuals are referred to as empaths.

Anywhere there is a crowd of people, there is abundant energy, both positive and negative. Those who assist with victim protection, do police or detective work, have served in war zones, operate as healers or psychics, or have careers at hospitals, clinics, or hospice centers deal with an overload of emotional energy from trying to help people. Many of them feel depleted, overwhelmed, nervous, depressed, or angry much of the time; they may feel as though someone is watching or following them, or have a difficult time finding peace of mind. Many of these individuals know that something is not quite "normal" since not everyone is adversely affected by going into public and not everyone picks up on the thoughts, feelings, or pain of those around them to such a degree. They may not know they are carrying or attaching to someone else's energy, but would love to stop the emotional, physical, and mental turmoil they encounter on a regular basis.

In her national bestseller, *The Highly Sensitive Person: How to Thrive When the World Overwhelms You,* author Elaine Aron, Ph.D. states that as many as one out of every five people are highly sensitive. And, no wonder! We live in an age when electronic information in the airwaves bombards us just about anywhere we go. We carry our cell phones, laptops, and other electronic devices with us on a daily basis. Our energetic field is infiltrated with background noise. While most people are able to tune it out or turn it down, some people have a difficult time processing this vast amount of energetic impulses. As a result they may have anxiety attacks, physical pain, or feel constantly weighed down, tired, or drained. Some may have an undiagnosed illness or pain. I believe the condition known as fibromyalgia—chronic pain that can ruin people's lives—is a result of sensory overload or negative energy being stored in the muscles. Dr. John Lowe-Houston also correlated fibromyalgia with an underactive thyroid problem, which leaves sensitive people tired and overwhelmed. In other words, empaths with fibromyalgia or hypothyroidism (or another illness) can become even *more* energy sensitive! Many doctors will tell their patients that this fatigued condition is just "in your head." But those doctors may not have considered how much our thoughts and emotions affect our physical health. Nor do they understand how repeatedly storing detrimental negative energy in the body and its surrounding energy field causes the vital life flow to become blocked or stagnant.

It is especially important for empaths to recognize their own energy and vibration, but many are not able to discern what their own energy feels like enough to know when it has roamed into someone's territory or when their own energy field is being violated. Most information you pick up from others is very routine or useless, so there's really no reason to carry it around. There are exercises in this book to help you learn to sense your own energy and let go of the rest.

If an empath does not understand what is happening he may think he is suffering from some form of mental distress or disorder. Psychology and psychiatry currently do not recognize empathy overload as an illness or know how to treat people who are suffering with this condition. While I am neither a doctor nor a psychologist, I am an empath and this empathic "gift" has both blessed and cursed my life. I have asked Dr. Caron B. Goode to join me in writing this book. Because she is a nationally certified counselor with membership in the American Psychotherapy Association, she is qualified to speak about the psychological issues regarding empathy and intuition. Her insight in chapter 7 will reveal the four basic core temperaments: Behavioral, Cognitive, Interpersonal, and Affective and answer questions such as *Does everyone have the ability or temperament to develop empathy? Or, are only specific people of certain temperaments prone to empathy? Are all children capable of empathy? How does empathy develop?* What Caron and I share with you in this book is intended to help you find a greater measure of inner peace by understanding a concept of the mind that perhaps no one has ever explained to you before.

An empath is sensitive to what is obvious (i.e.: body language, gestures, or tone of voice), as well as unseen things such as the thoughts, emotions, and illnesses they sense in another person. Empaths may get hunches, see mental pictures, hear voices, or have a gut feeling that supplies hidden information about people and situations. They may also get a physical sensation in their body that lets them know where another person is afflicted or suffering.

Because empathy is part of our overall divine guidance system (known as intuition), I may use empathy and intuition interchangeably throughout this book. However, there is a distinction between the two: intuition is a spiritual gift that gives us the ability to "read" people and situations and "know" things that have not been disclosed to us. It also gives impartial and unemotional direction to make life easier if its instructions are followed. Empathy is the ability to show concern for people; it allows us to pick up information and process it through sight, sound, touch, smell, and taste. Untrained empaths can go too far in trying to lessen the burdens of others by carrying their emotion or pain *for* them.

Both intuition and empathy allow us to access mental and emotional information that has not been verbally communicated. We might consider them to be psychic abilities, extra-sensory perception (ESP), or a sixth sense. Like the language of our dreams, messages from the unconscious mind have to be heeded or interpreted in order to make sense. Untrained empaths who ignore, resist, or refuse to deal with the energy they are submersed into find themselves consumed and overwhelmed by it. They must learn to wisely employ the gift of empathy as part of their overall guidance system. There is little material on how to do this. Therefore, Caron and I believe this book will benefit many people and help get them moving toward better health. By being led to this book, you obviously have some need for understanding of what is going on in your mind, emotions, and body. Great news! You are not crazy; you have simply been unaware of how you are affected by energy overload.

There are plenty of well-adjusted and fully-developed empaths in our world, including Dr. Goode and her husband, Tom. In this book, I plan to introduce you to some of the empaths I met during my research and demonstrate how our empathy can become a blessing rather than a nuisance. I have included a resources section at the end of this book to help you get in touch with energy workers and trained empaths, and find books, tools, and groups to help you take the next step.

Developing intuition and empathic abilities is a journey of self-discovery that can awaken you to an entirely new understanding about life and what you currently believe about yourself. The more we embrace the fact that we are spiritually, mentally, and emotionally connected to one another, the more responsible we must become in managing our personal energy and our electromagnetic field. Everything we think, say, or do affects all of humanity and ultimately our planet. Let's join together in a better understanding of this connection by managing the gift of empathy and developing trustworthy intuition.

Chapter 1 ~ What Is an Empath?

My mother once said to my ex-husband, "Yvonne is the weak one in the family. She's emotionally sensitive and has always cried a lot." What she meant, but didn't have language to express, is that her daughter is an empath. I did cry a lot before I knew how to prevent myself from carrying the energetic burdens of others, but I could not have been weak or would never have made it this far!

Like me, perhaps you were told by the teachers and adults around you that you are "overly or too sensitive." Perhaps they didn't know you had the gift of empathy. Empathy is the ability to feel what another person, animal, or spirit is feeling—to put yourself in their shoes so to speak—or into their pain, suffering, depression, illness, etc. An empath is a person who uses emotional intuition to understand or connect with others. Children naturally have this ability. At birth we have shapeless borders. We move our energy fields (aura) in and around the energy fields of other people in order to check out how they are feeling. We instinctively do this in order to get what we want, be safe, or understand our environment. Adults provide a role model that demonstrates how to hide our true feelings. Adults are quick to shush a child who "tells the truth" on adults, predicts the future, proclaims to see ghosts, or has recurring aches or illnesses that can't be medically explained. As children age, they learn to live with pain rather than live authentically and use their intuition to better their lives.

Thoughts, feelings, and beliefs are a subtle form of energy. Through quantum physics, it has been scientifically proven that everything—even items that seem to be solid—when viewed at an atomic or subatomic level is energy manifested in different forms, states, and frequencies. We are submersed in a matrix or field of intelligent energy. Max Planck first proposed the quantum theory of an energy matrix in 1944. Today, scientists agree that everything—even what we once thought to be empty space—is actually comprised of particles and waves of energy. We are much more powerful than we realize. Not only are we affected by this ever-changing field of energy, our DNA, thoughts, feelings, and beliefs can rearrange the field as we interact with one another.

How can we *not* be affected by other people's energy? It only seems natural. As spirit or energy, we are all empathic to some degree, but some people have the uncanny ability to feel energy more easily and intensely than the average person. Some even feel the physical pain of others. At times, this ability can disrupt empaths' lives because they become emotionally drained or physically ill as a result of trying to carry someone else's energy along with their own. Many times empaths are unable to identify or separate their own energy from that of another person. These energy-sensitive people are the empaths to whom this book is geared.

We are all born with the ability to tap into another person's energy field to receive impulses, perceive intention, or project our thoughts and influence on others. Even though you may not recognize this ability as a psychic skill, you've probably "felt" someone else's energy. For example, have you ever been sitting in a public place—perhaps reading a book and minding your own business—and sensed that someone was projecting energy toward you? When you looked up, you caught someone staring at you from across the room.

According to Elaine N. Aron, Ph.D, between fifteen and twenty percent of the population are empaths—she calls them a "highly sensitive person" (HSP)—who have an excess amount of sentient ability. They tend to become overloaded with the psychic energy of others to the point of compromising their own well-being. They feel drained, tired, or emotionally distressed as they pick up on every kind of sickness. From time to time, empaths are overwhelmed by the emotional information they receive from everyone around them—including friends, family members, and strangers. Some can even sense the emotions of those who are in another city, state, or country. Many times the information is scrambled like a radio station; and since the messages come from a variety of sources, it may be difficult for empaths to discern whose energy they are picking up on. This can cause depression, anxiety attacks, physical symptoms, or a burst of emotions that seem to appear for no reason. Most empaths have no idea how to manage this energy or turn it off. Some don't even know they *are* an empath, much less what to do about it. This condition is compounded when an empath does not recognize how his or her own energy feels or is disconnected from his or her own body, thoughts, and feelings. You may be one of them.

Being empathic is not a burden you must bear anymore. You can learn to shut out unwanted energy and keep others from violating your personal boundaries. First, you have to set boundaries. I will show you how to do that in the upcoming chapters. You can also learn to direct your own energy and keep it from "leaking" or roaming by default. Then you will be able to send healing vibes when *you* choose rather than when someone wants to siphon your energy. You may find that you have undeveloped psychic gifts that you want to hone. It is possible to tap into another person's field *when invited* to read the emotional information and help them know what is going on energetically for them.

I will share my personal story in this book because it is an unusual one, but one that many empaths will relate to. If I can help one person avoid what I went through, it will be worth the effort it took to write this book. For those who feel stuck, helpless, and desperate, there is hope. If I can come out of the horrible state of despair I was in, so can you.

For years while in the constraints of organized religions, I didn't know I was an empath. I had never heard the term, but I tried to help people understand and accept my spiritual "gift." Those who witnessed my intercessory prayer efforts didn't understand what was going on and very few desired to pray with the intensity that I did. I still wonder how many prayer warriors are empaths who simply don't know why they have mysterious illnesses and feel drained all the time. When I let the word out that I was writing a book on this topic, people started coming out of the woodwork, asking questions, relating their "ah ha" moments, and willing to share their stories as empaths. Alas, I found that we empaths are plenteous in number!

As I felt more comfortable with who I am and learned to manage energy, I realized I could actually help empaths who are just beginning to realize that they are tapping into other people's pain, suffering, drama, illnesses, and injuries. Perhaps I could teach empaths what I have learned the hard way so they could avoid misery that comes from lack of knowledge. I decided to share my spiritual practices and coping methods because I know they work. To illustrate points of discussion and carry the message of hope to those who can't relate to my Christian-prayer-warrior-turned-metaphysician background, I collected insight from empaths who have walked a different path. I have also researched this topic to find out what the experts are saying about empathy. My utmost intention is to help you find healing by recognizing your own energy and preventing random energetic exchanges that occur without your conscious awareness. I will teach you how to raise your vibration and connect with spirit teachers in higher realms, making you less attractive to lower level energies. By setting healthy boundaries and developing emotional intelligence, you can manage your own energy and discern what others are feeling without actually having to suffer for it! In fact, with a little more information, you will be able to turn this "curse" into a gift that can ease the emotional and physical pain of others.

Chapter 2 ~ Characteristics of An Untrained Empath

"What's wrong with me, doc?" I asked as I sat on the examination table in the emergency room of a clinic in Muncie, Indiana. "My heart is pounding, my head is spinning, and I feel like I'm going to pass out. I haven't done anything out of the norm."

"I can't find a thing wrong with you," he said. "You must be having an anxiety attack or allergic reaction to something."

"I had a root canal last week and nearly fainted. The dentist said I am allergic to Novocain. Could that be it?"

"Have you had these symptoms continuously since then?"

"No, they came up suddenly this afternoon."

"Are you taking any kind of medication?"

"Nothing but Tylenol. I still have a headache."

"What were you doing when the symptoms started?"

"Praying."

The doctor had no explanation. He gave me some Benadryl and sent me home. I slept the rest of the day.

My symptoms were energetically related. Most medical doctors do not understand how the energy from one person can affect another person and cause physical pain or emotional distress.

Before I had a label to put on my empathetic ability, I called myself an intercessor or "surrogate" for carrying the burdens of others to the throne of grace—a noble and worthy cause. As I prayed for the entire city on a daily basis, I picked up on the energy of thousands of people and took on the suffering of many of them. However, I didn't realize what was happening until it nearly killed me.

Emotions such as fear, anger, and frustration are energies. Like a virus, you can potentially "catch" them from people without realizing it. Empathic people can be psychic sponges that absorb energy everywhere they go. I was so energy sensitive that if I heard an ambulance siren, I would feel instant panic. If I came upon an accident scene or a homeless person, I cried. If I saw an open wound, I would feel an electric shock all over my body. In traffic, I felt the anger and frustration of my fellow drivers so bad that my throat would close up and I could not swallow. When I was in my prayer closet, I would cry, groan, shake, and travail on behalf of others. These and similar scenarios were so common for me that I thought everyone felt this way. I had no idea that I was an empath. I had never heard of such a thing.

Webster defines empathy as "the capacity for participation in another person's feelings." Everyone has some empathic ability. We were all born with the ability to feel other people's emotions, thoughts, and physical sensations. We may get intuitive clues about a person and feel that we cannot trust him or feel that he is hiding something or lying. We can listen to our intuition about a situation and ascertain whether or not it is safe or wise for us to proceed. Being able to know what others are thinking, feeling, or experiencing is a way of protecting ourselves. It also has its drawbacks when unchecked.

While shopping at Wal-Mart one day I suddenly had a panic attack. Fear overtook my body and the "fight or flight" adrenaline rush nearly crippled me as I clung to the shopping cart. I felt as though I was going to pass out before I could get to a place where I could sit down. I was shaking so hard, I could hardly breathe. My heart was pounding fiercely and at first I thought I was having a heart attack! Within one minute a "Code Adam" announcement came over the store's intercom system and the store was locked down. I knew then that I had taken into my body and emotions the panic and fear of the parent who had lost their child in the store. Fortunately, I was still able to sense my own personal energy separate from this chaos. Part of me was calm and level-headed as I witnessed this bizarre emotional reaction. I was sane enough to call upon angels to help locate the boy and reunite him safely with his parent—I intuitively knew the child was male and that his mother was in the store. I placed myself inside a bubble of protection—a visual exercise I use for protection—and the symptoms began subsiding. When I heard the child had been found, I cried for joy. I knew I was still picking up on the mother's energy of relief, but that was the best I could do at the time. I immediately left my cart in the aisle and walked out of the store. I was wiped out for the rest of the day.

I opened an email not too long ago and sensed the hateful energy of the person who sent it. But, it did not cause me undue alarm. I was able to write a calm response to the sender and gently set boundaries and keep peace in our relationship. Why such a change? Because I now recognize my own energy well enough that 90 percent of the time I can tell when I'm picking up on someone else's stuff. Plus, I have boundaries in place that protect my energy field. So, I'm not as apt to be "hit" by the info-energy of my environment or the wandering thoughts of those who do not have reins on their personal energy. That's not to say that I don't get surprised from time to time, but at least I now have tools to clear the energy and not let it get to me the way it once did.

Empaths are loving, caring, kind people who want to help others. They are often found doing volunteer work and may serve others through emotionally-demanding careers as childcare givers, medical professionals, hospice workers, midwives, and such. Most empaths came in with a mission to heal people, animals, plants, and the planet. As healers, many have taken on so much external energy that they spend most of their time trying to clear unwanted energy and recuperate from the last episode that "blew their doors off."

Peace and joy are natural characteristics of human beings, but because empaths want to heal others and make everyone happy, they tend to absorb negative energy such as fear, depression, or rage instead. Empaths may feel responsible for other people's happiness and try to fix things that are wrong in other people's relationships, physical bodies, and even the world. This makes empaths particularly easy targets for emotional vampires—those who don't want to take responsibility for their own choices and seek someone to do everything for them.

Here are a few characteristics of empaths who have not learned to filter out other people's emotions or manage their own energy:

- You constantly feel overwhelmed with emotions and you may cry a lot, feel sad, angry, or depressed for no good reason. You may be tempted to think you are crazy for having random mood swings and bouts of unexplained fatigue. If you are a woman, it's like having PMS all the time! Unrestrained empathy can cause a person to manifest symptoms similar to bipolar (manic-depressive) disorder.

- You drop by the store feeling great, but once you get in a crowd you start feeling down, angry, sad, or overwhelmed. You feel you must be coming down with something so you decide to go home and rest.

- If you've found that you can't be in public without becoming overwhelmed you may start to live the life of a hermit. But, even at home, you get depressed when you watch the news and you cry while watching a movie. You feel horrible when a commercial for the Humane Society shows animals that need a home. You may rescue more animals than you can possibly care for.

- You feel sorry for people no matter who they are or what they have done. You feel the need to stop and help anyone in your path. You can't pass by a homeless person without giving him money— even if you don't have it to spare.

- Many empaths are overweight. When they absorb stressful emotions, it can trigger panic attacks, depression as well as food, sex, and drug binges. Some may overeat to cope with emotional stress or use their body weight as a shield or buffer. In Chapter 9 I will show you how to use light as your protection.

- Most empaths have the ability to physically and emotionally heal others by drawing the pain or ailment out of the sick person and into their own bodies. For obvious reasons, this is not recommended unless you know how to keep from becoming ill in the process.

- From chest pains and stomach cramps to migraines and fever, you manifest symptoms without contracting an actual illness. Later, you learn that your "ailment" coincided with the onset of a friend or family member's illness.

- No one can lie to you because you can see through their façade and know what they really mean. You may even know *why* they lied.

- People—even strangers—open up and start volunteering their personal information. You may be sitting in the waiting room minding your own business and waiting your turn when the person next to you starts sharing all kinds of personal information. You didn't ask them to and they never considered that you might not want to hear about their drama. People may feel better after speaking with you, but you end up feeling worse because they have transferred their emotional pain to you.

- Some empaths don't do well with intimate relationships. Constantly taking on their partner's pain and emotions, they may easily get their feelings hurt, desire to spend time alone rather than with the partner, feel vulnerable when having sex, and feel that they have to continually retrieve their own energy when it gets jumbled with that of their partner. They may be so afraid of becoming engulfed by another person that they close up emotionally just to survive.

- The ill, the suffering, and those with weak boundaries are drawn to the unconditional understanding and compassion an empath emits without even being aware of it. Until you learn how to shut out the energy of others, you may have a pretty miserable existence in which you feel like you have to be entirely alone in order to survive.

It's easy to see why being an empath is often very draining. No wonder that over time, some folks shut down their empathic ability. Like the Patrick Jane character in *The Mentalist*, they may deny they are psychic and use other clues to get emotional information (such as body language and non-verbal indicators). There is no need to build walls and shut down your awareness or intuition. Instead, you can shift from feeling the energy inside your body/emotions and begin to perceive it as external energetic impulses that have a message for you.

Chapter 3 ~ My Personal Story

I share my background to show how out of balance my life once was due to being an empath. My personal experience shows some unusual ways empathy operated in my life as an intercessor prayer "warrior." Regardless of whether you consider yourself a spiritual or religious person, I'm certain you will find application to how empathy is operating in your life. My goal is to help you avoid the trauma I experienced and to teach you how to stay healthy in your own body, mind, and emotions. While I cared for people through prayer, you may care for them physically through your work as a nurse, hospice volunteer, medical professional, or some other service-oriented occupation.

For the first forty years of my life I was enmeshed with the fundamental dogma of the Baptist church and I lived according to the interpretation of the Bible that my family, society, and the church passed down to me. I was manifesting the spiritual gifts outlined in I Corinthians 12, but no one in our church seemed to believe in the gifts, much less help me develop them.

I'll quote the New International Version of I Corinthians 12: 1-11 for those who are not familiar with this scripture.[1]

> *There are different kinds of gifts, but the same Spirit. There are different kinds of service, but the same Lord. There are different kinds of*

working, but the same God works all of them in all men.

*Now to each one the manifestation of the Spirit is given for the common good. To one there is given through the Spirit the **message of wisdom**, to another the **message of knowledge** by means of the same Spirit, to another **faith** by the same Spirit, to another **gifts of healing** by that one Spirit, to another **miraculous powers**, to another **prophecy**, to another **distinguishing between spirits**, to another **speaking in different kinds of tongues**, and to still another the **interpretation of tongues**. All these are the work of one and the same Spirit, and he gives them to each one, just as he determines.*

Empaths have psychic abilities or spiritual gifts referred to as clairsentience (physical or gut feeling or a "knowing"), clairvoyance (seeing visions) or clairaudience (hearing voices). There is really no difference between these three; they are products of intuition or empathy. The only difference is in how the brain decides to process the information.

Clairsentience has two aspects: knowing and feeling. A clairsentient person may pick up a thought and "know" something without having prior information about another person or situation (*message of knowledge or wisdom*). This precognitive aspect of the gift may come as hunches, dreams, gut feelings, and knowings that predict future events that happen in reality, or insight into present situations (*prophecy*). A person with the feeling aspect of the clairsentient gift can pick up a thought and transform it into a feeling. They can also heal others in this manner.

Clairaudience has to do with hearing. A clairaudient person may pick up an energetic impulse from another person's thought and hear it either internally in their mind or as an audible voice.

Clairvoyance has to do with vision. When the brain picks up a thought impulse, it is transmitted as a vision, symbol, image, or color using the mind's eye. The clairvoyant may have the ability to read auras—the energy surrounding a person, animal, or object—or see chakras. We will discuss auras and chakras later in this book.

A type of energetic communication is employed whenever empathy is in operation. This subconscious or telepathic connection is what transfers information when you tap into the thoughts, feelings, or illnesses of others—even those of spirits that do not have a physical body (*distinguishing between spirits*). Unfortunately, our society, Hollywood movies, and religious programming have caused many to believe that the unseen realm either does not exist or is something to be terribly afraid of. None of these sources can be trusted when the present ideas that conflict with your personal experience.

Empaths already possess the ability to pick up non-verbal information. I foresee a day when we will all be able to read one another's minds, which means some of us are going to be quite embarrassed when we are unable to lie to one another. I share this recent story to show you how innocently and easily telepathy operates.

As my husband handed me a letter, he said, "Guess who I saw today?"

Looking at the return address I thought it read, Hughes. "Wow! I haven't heard from Leslee in a long time," I said as I opened the letter. It was from a client named Hinkes. Bewildered at how I could have seen Hughes on the envelope, I laid it aside and asked my husband, "So, who did you see today?"

"You just said her name. I saw Leslee Hughes."

I had telepathically retrieved her name from my husband's mind. My third eye confirmed the answer by causing my physical eyes to see her name on the envelope. Empathic people can increase this telepathic ability as they develop their intuition.

Fear keeps us in bondage to many false ideas and beliefs. Fear kept one religion from recognizing the evolution of man until 1996. And, even though the Pythagorean philosopher Philolaus (d. 390 BC) first speculated that the Earth was round and that the planets revolved around the sun rather than the Earth, the Catholic Church refused to believe it until 1992.[2] I'm stating this to remind you to not let your fear of psychic or spiritual gifts keep you from accepting and trusting your intuition and using telepathy and empathy as a valuable tools for navigating life on Earth. Sometimes our experiences have to take precedence over what is taught in any text—sacred or otherwise. To keep believing something you've been taught when it is not validated by your personal experience is to live inauthentic to your own truth. This type of programming is what shuts down the voice of inner guidance and causes us to distrust our intuition.

Back to my story. When we moved twenty miles from our families of origin, my husband (now my ex) was away on business even more than he had been prior. As the newly installed head of household I had the perfect opportunity to find community in an environment where the gifts of the Spirit were accepted to a greater degree. So, my teenage children and I began fellowshipping with Lawrenceville Church of God, which was part of the Pentecostal denomination headquartered in Cleveland, Tennessee. With my husband away much of the time, it was not uncommon for me to be locked away in my prayer room for hours each day, singing, playing keyboards, writing worship songs, interceding, and laying in trance until my kids were home from school or ready for dinner.

Seeking to experience more of the spiritual gifts—especially that of healing—I fasted on a regular basis and prayed for the manifestation of these gifts. From what I understand about fasting, it raises the body's vibration and enables one to interact with beings in higher spiritual realms. I really had a dilemma when I experienced an increase in all nine spiritual gifts. Some people thought I was crazy for revealing that I was having prophetic dreams and visions or that I saw, sensed, felt, and heard ghosts. I even smelled and tasted things that no one else did. Miracles and healing began occurring as answered prayer. I prayed in several different "tongues" that actually sounded like distinct languages rather than incoherent babbling. Many times I intuitively knew what I was praying. I was aware of spirit beings around me, and knew things about people that I had not been told. To say the least, I was no longer the "normal" churchgoer even in the Pentecostal religion that I thought would be more accepting of spiritual gifts.

My ex-husband's job transferred our family to Muncie, Indiana in 1997, offering him the opportunity to cease traveling and be home with his family. While that promise did not pan out (he traveled just as much if not more), we joined a spirit-filled Methodist church and quickly put down roots. I became involved in multiple prayer groups among a wide range of denominations throughout the city. Leading worship from my keyboard during private and public prayer vigils, I regularly experienced uncontrollable sobbing, shaking, jerking, moaning, and groaning or overwhelming joy, laughter, and a feeling that I needed to dance or move my body just to release some of the energy I was connecting with.

This was during a time when a movement known as the "Toronto Blessing," which began at the Toronto Airport Vineyard in January, 1994, was gaining recognition in Pentecostal circles. My manifestations were accepted as normal in this renewal movement and I was delighted to find about half a dozen people who not only understood my spiritual gifts but also manifested the "symptoms" as we prayed together on Tuesday nights. One precious man had a mature understanding of spiritual gifts and mentioned us in giving prophetic readings to one another. While he did not know about empathy as it is mentioned in this book, he did advise us to put up protective barriers to "keep Satan and his demons out." This defensive, resistant stance only increased my interaction with dark entities, who were all too willing to play along with my ignorance. I was picking up energy not only from humans but also from disembodied spirits. I thought I was doing a good thing and actually driving out these evil entities, but by focusing on evil, the negative energy I was drawing to myself intensified. Having accidents, being verbally attacked, and even cursed by others, I thought I was giving Satan a run for his money. I knew little about protecting myself from the depression, anxiety, fear, addictions, suicidal tendencies, phobias, relationship difficulties, and other problems caused by entity contamination. Because I believed I was pleasing God with my emotional suffering, I counted it all joy and continued on! I didn't realize how this effort was draining the very life out of me.

Much confusion surrounds the topic of demons and whether or not they are real, but what I experienced while I held this fear-based mindset had an impact on my well-being. Empaths are extremely sensitive to any kind of energy—even that of our own thoughts and beliefs.

An entity is anything that feeds off your energy or emotions. It can be a thought form, an energy pattern, or a soul tie (a hook to or an attachment from one or more persons), or an earthbound spirit no longer in a human body. Whatever beliefs, emotions, or knowledge we have when we leave the body is carried with the soul into the afterlife. Many times when a soul leaves the body abruptly, it is confused and may not cross over to the other side or go into the light. These spirits are between incarnations and able to feed off the energy of humans.

I don't believe a body can be possessed by more than one soul at a time, but we can be influenced positively or negatively by disembodied souls. I don't intend to make anyone afraid—you are more powerful than any earthbound spirit and they have to adhere to any boundary you set with them—but if you are an empath, there is a good chance you see ghosts, or have already experienced some evidence that they exist. Obviously, we are connected to one another or we would not be able to tap into one another's energy like we do. Incarnated or disembodied, we are all interconnected in ways that we may or may not have acknowledged or

39

understood. I'll talk more about this in chapter 10 under the subheading "Setting Boundaries with Entities."

Our lesson here is that whatever we think about comes about. The universe will allow us to feel or experience whatever we validate as truth. The great news is that all entities (real or imagined) can be removed with better understanding. Doing the clearing and cleansing practices mentioned in Chapter 9 will help immensely.

My husband didn't know what to think of the strange occurrences that I was finally brave enough to share with him, and as much as he wanted to support me, he just couldn't appreciate the peculiar manifestations I was exhibiting. He tolerated it the best he could when he personally felt energy flowing when we prayed together. Others felt it too. Along with being the one was who was swooning or falling backward—a practice Pentecostals call being "slain in the Spirit"—those I laid hands on and prayed for were also falling down in a trance-like state. Sensing I had the anointing of a healer, I began facilitating healing events like a modern-day Kathryn Kuhlman and witnessed miraculous results with people being healed both physically and emotionally.

That "happy" season ended in late 1997 when my husband's job required yet another relocation of our family—this time to Nashville, Tennessee where he would be working in the home office. The promise that he would be home a lot more became a reality. However, having him home every night caused me to recognize just how different our views about spiritual things really were. He became aware of how many hours I was spending in the prayer closet and just how much I was crying and acting—well . . . just plain weird.

I could not expect my husband to be a reclusive intercessor like me, and he could not expect me to be the socialite wife who would hang on his arm while he ascended the corporate ladder.

In an attempt to reconcile our differences, we tried many nondenominational churches that promised an acceptance of the spiritual gifts that I had become quite comfortable with, but I could not find a ministry in Music City that would allow me to participate musically. There seemed to be no intercessors like I had known in Muncie. We settled on one just to have a church home and find some much needed fellowship. The loneliness and emptiness I felt inside was horrible and I became extremely depressed.

Nearly forty years of co-dependency, repressed feelings, legalistic religion, and fifteen or more years of carrying the burdens of others through intercession (empathy) were demanding to be dealt with and released, but I managed to keep my problems to myself until I emotionally fell apart in my grandmother's bathroom on Thanksgiving Day that year. While I was sobbing my heart out to my mother, my grandmother gave her two cents worth, "Just hold your chin up and keep praying. Be strong and keep your faith in God. Don't let this get you down." Hmmm . . . pray more? *Really*?

Needless to say, all this turmoil took its toll on my marriage; and divorce—a non-Christian act I had vowed never to participate in—became a harsh reality. Even though my husband and I sought counseling, we finally had to face the fact that our marriage had died many years prior and it was time to bury it and move on. Some of our religious friends judged us for not being able to save our marriage. One person in our small Bible study group told me I should have prayed more! If she only knew . . .

By then, I had serious doubts that God even existed and I questioned everything my religion had taught me. I had no one to talk to about my personal problems but inwardly I began to reevaluate my entire life. I needed to heal not only from my divorce, but also from religious addiction to prayer. Walking through a mental and emotional fog, I felt like I had been kicked out of heaven. I tried to pray, but found that I could no longer intercede with the fervor and intensity that I had before. Looking back, I'm thankful I stopped before it killed *my body*. It *did* create the opportunity for the soul that originally incarnated into this body to walk out and the spirit that I am now (LavendarRose) to walk in. This event is known as a soul exchange. I won't get into any detail about it here, but I do plan to write and publish a book about my life-transforming experience. So, stayed tuned!

Even though I was angry with myself for having empathetic gifts, I knew there was a way to use them to help others. But I would have to understand them from a new perspective because I was never going back to church—never, ever!

Sources for Chapter 3:

1. New International Version of the Holy Bible. Zondervan, 1985.

2. "Galileo Galilei." <u>Wikipedia.com</u>. Accessed 22 November 2010. <http://en.wikipedia.org/wiki/Galileo_Galilei>.

Chapter 4 ~ Turning Point

"Never, ever" came around much sooner than I anticipated. I had one more mission to perform that would totally change my life and lead me to the answers of many questions I had about my empathic experiences.

My divorce proceedings were still pending when my spiritual guidance led me to a church where I met my current husband, a musician and worship leader named Randy. Since I was neither looking for a husband nor a church, I let Randy know up front about my bizarre spiritual gifts. He had no issue with them and would allow me to spend time in intercessory prayer, which he believed strongly in. He also had prophetic dreams and visions, and had seen in the spirit realm; (I later learned that he had seen me in a vision and knew when we met that I was going to one day be his wife); therefore, I was in good company and felt safe with him. Regardless of whether it was divinely inspired or a total lack of common sense, he and I married ten weeks after we met.

I immediately noticed that this non-denominational church we were attending was just as outlandish in its teachings as all the fundamentalist churches I had attended. I had left these types of churches four times (three churches—the same one twice, under a different pastor). Attending church really went against my better judgment, but I stayed because I had a strong desire to use my spiritual gifts in service to others. However, before I could minister at this church, I would have to jump through all the hoops, take several classes, and prove myself to the new congregation and leadership before I could even become a member.

During the entire year I spent trying to heal from my past relationship and bond with my new husband, I kept waiting for the chance to break away from the doctrine and dogma coming from the pulpit. And finally that day came. Randy and I agreed to leave the fellowship when we commanded to obey a mandate given by a pastor whose leadership we no longer trusted.

That expulsion led us both on a deeper search for truth that aligned with our experience and had no rules or regulations to follow. Together we read books, listened to CDs, attended psychic fairs and workshops, and devoured information about dreams, visions, past lives, chakras, energy work, reincarnation, animal totems, quantum physics, higher planes of consciousness, and anything that would show us something other than what we had been taught in Christian circles. Through correspondence courses at the American Institute of Holistic Theology, we both earned our bachelor of science in metaphysics. Randy later earned his master's degree.

While we were reprogramming our minds and healing our emotions, I stopped all forms of intercession and worship. I gave away my keyboard and my piano. Even though I no longer sought a public place to use my spiritual gifts, I continued to have unsolicited visitations from disembodied spirits and I continued to carry energetic burdens for my children and family members. When my sister-in-law's mother was dying of liver cancer, I prayed for her recovery. When I began experiencing symptoms similar to hers, I realized what was happening. I was carrying her burden of physical illness. I immediately stopped praying for her, she died, and my symptoms ceased.

Realizing that being an empath was having a detrimental effect upon me, I used some of the methods I describe in Chapter 9 to keep from picking up the energy of others who were in my presence, but there were still times when I was broadsided—like the time when our friends, Sally and Angie, were at our house having dinner with me and Randy. I was talking about my work as a writer when all of a sudden my throat closed up and a stabbing pain hit me in my neck and upper chest. I grabbed my throat in a panic that caused Randy and Angie to think I was choking. I couldn't swallow or speak to tell them what was wrong. Thankfully, Sally is an intuitive healer and recognized that I was not choking, but needed to be released from a psychic energy attack. She worked to clear me and when I could speak again, I had insight as to what had just happened. I had been considering ghostwriting a book for a man whose father had witnessed the assassination of President Kennedy. He was about to report the culprit to the authorities when he was attacked from behind, stabbed in the throat, and left to die in an alley. The client wanted me to write about what his father had shared with him prior to his death. I had picked up the traumatic energy of a ghost!

That event was a big eye-opener for me. This business of being an empath had gone too far and it had to stop for good. I adopted new ways to protect myself with grounding and centering exercises that I will share in Chapter 9. I meditated to receive energy from higher realms and learned how to run my own energy through my chakras. If I prayed for anyone, I detached myself from the person's energy and did not allow myself to become emotionally involved.

I also detached from the outcome of my prayers. I would offer the energy of healing, but I no longer attempted to know the plan for another person's soul. I refused to usurp the free will of others as I had many times in my religious prayer efforts when I was trying to save the world. Instead, I started sending people divine love and light—an energy that they could use however they and God chose. Since I was directing a higher energy rather than sending out my own energy, I was not taking on the detrimental energy my prayer recipients were releasing from their blocked chakras or cells.

When I stopped using my own energy to offer healing to others, the empathic attacks lessened, but I was still able to see and hear in the spirit realm. Disembodied souls would awaken me during the night and hover overhead, starring at me until I woke up. I heard things no one else heard and I could feel the energy of ghosts around me. I even wrote a book about it, *More Than Meets the Eye True Stories About Death, Dying, and Afterlife*.

Jerry, a friend of mine, was fatally stabbed in the parking lot of a Kroger store in 2007 while trying to stop a man who had stolen a purse from a 60-year-old woman. When I heard Jerry had died, I was immediately catapulted into an empathetic episode like I had not experienced since I was serving as an intercessory prayer warrior in the city of Muncie in the mid-1990s. The grief-like energy I was carrying for Jerry's friends and family was so severe that after two days, I finally called on an energy-worker friend, Cherise Thorne, to clear me so I could stop sobbing.

After that, I put up some really strong protective barriers to keep from taking on other people's energy, but Jerry didn't seem to get the message. His spirit hung around me for more than a week following his death. I didn't want to do what he was urging me to do contact his mom and sister (Dianne) and give them a message from him: "Tell them I am with Mason." The message didn't mean anything to me. I wasn't sure if Mason was a person, a pet, a bricklayer, or a lodge member. I hesitated sharing this insight because I didn't know how open his sister and mom were to having a stranger give them a psychic message and I didn't want to add to their grief. What if I was wrong and the message had no relevance to them? However, Jerry was insistent and at the time, I didn't know how to make ghosts go away. So, I found his mother's address and wrote a letter giving her the message with my phone number and return address. I didn't hear anything from the family until early two and a half years later when I got a letter from his sister, stating that she finally knew what the message meant.

When the spirits started moving objects and breaking things in my house, I drew the line. Enough of this intrusion of my personal space! I pretty much shut down my contact with the spirit world and focused my energy on my writing and editing business. I used the archangel technique described in Chapter 9 and stopped having intrusive spirits around me. I was fully retired as an empath!

I lived in a vibratory frequency above the fearful "what ifs" and drama of Earth life and was doing pretty good until the first weekend in May 2010 brought an event to Nashville that those who were here will never forget. We knew we were in for some heavy storms, but we had no idea we were about to be flooded by a deluge of water that would swell rivers, lakes, and creeks to the point that more than 9,600 homes, in addition to hundreds of businesses, vehicles, livestock, and human lives, were destroyed. As twenty inches of rain fell in about twelve hours, the rivers rose and kept rising for two days until they crested at about fifty feet above average.

People were evacuated, some were rescued by boat, and others were without electricity and stuck on their side of the road where bridges and roadways had washed out. Business and tourism was called to a halt as people tried to take in the shock of what had happened. Only when the waters receded enough for residents to return home, did they realize how bad the situation really was. One of the city's two water treatment plants was damaged and unable to operate for more than ten days, so all of Davidson County was put on a mandatory 50 percent reduction of water usage. My grandson's elementary school was flooded with contaminated water at a level that reached almost to the ceiling. The 2009-2010 school year was brought to an early end. Music City was declared a state of emergency and FEMA was called in to assist. There were billions of dollars worth of damage, twenty-seven lives lost, and homes completely swept off their foundation and pushed down the street by a raging current like something you might see in a horror movie. But the horror was real.

You can imagine how this affected those who are spiritually sensitive to the suffering of others or of Mother Gaia herself. For several weeks prior to the flood, my daughter-in-law felt angry but was puzzled as to why. Once the flood came, she felt a release and was calm again. She had been taking on the geophysical feelings of the Mother planet as she responded to our blatant misuse of her resources. The BP oil spill in the Gulf of Mexico was occurring during our catastrophe in Nashville.

My emotional empathy began the day after the storm. I began feeling depressed and sad—almost to the point of tears, even though our property and lives had not been affected. I thought the sudden rush of emotions had something to do with being an empath and connecting with the many Nashvillians who were experiencing loss, but I had resigned from that role and was no longer in the business of carrying other people's negative energy as my own. Or, so I thought.

The strong feelings of sorrow and helplessness continued to increase. I found a way to release some of the energy by becoming a clearing house for posting information online to help people know about community meetings, donation stations, and other events to help victims and volunteers find one another. Having that outlet helped a lot but I still continued to have underlying feelings of depression. That's when the phone calls and emails started. People I had not heard from in a while started sending encouraging emails saying they were thinking about me. One woman left me uplifting voice messages (I had retreated so much that I was not even answering my phone) to say she was sending me love and light. That made a huge difference. These prayers and positive energy helped clear me of most of the despair I was feeling, but I was still not back to my usual jovial self.

To make matters worse, my writing business was taking a hit. The business had been flourishing all year and I actually had leads "flooding" in so fast and heavy that I was scrambling to train and bring on new team members to help carry the load. After the Nashville flood, all leads stopped instantly. For three weeks not a single person requested our writing or editing services. I was shocked because this had not happened in years. Trying to figure out why I was so down, only made the symptoms worse.

Within about a week, my emotional stamina had declined to where I had no desire to get out of bed in the morning. I didn't want to go to my office and hunt for a lead. I sensed it was time for me to just rest, relax, and meditate to get clarity on how to I transform my life through this process, but I had no desire to do anything but eat, watch TV, and play games on my laptop. I had to be *doing* something to keep my mind from worrying about my finances, business, and emotional and physical health.

One Saturday morning, my husband decided he had watched me mope about long enough. He knew there was a spiritual cause for my emotional despair, so he insisted that I allow him to perform Hands of Light (a technique taught by Barbara Ann Brennan) energy work on me. After he opened and restored balance to my energy centers (chakras), my emotions returned to normal by the end of the day. By Monday, I was cheerful, hopeful, joyful, and I had a sense that my business was about to take a shift that would move me toward bringing my spiritual knowledge into my business endeavors that had been taking most of my time and attention. While I was still meditating and using protective measures, I had not been focusing on developing my psychic skills.

I had a feeling that this shift might mean I would have to reopen the gift of empathy. The universe knew I would not be easily talked into that; so, they sent multiple confirmations that allowed me to rest, relax, and restore.

First, I found a bird feather on my back porch. As I picked it up, I heard my spirit say, "blue jay." Not being much of an expert on birds, I did some research, which meant taking a photo of the feather and posting it on Twitter. Within a few minutes someone confirmed it was indeed a blue jay feather. So, I got out Ted Andrews' *Animal Speak* book and here's an excerpt of what I found.

> *For those to whom the jay comes as a totem, it can reflect lessons in using your own power properly. It can also reflect lessons in not allowing yourself to be placed a position in which power is misused against you.*
>
> *The jay has the ability to access the heavens and earth for greater power. This totem can move between both worlds and tap the primal energies at either level. The main problem will be in dabbling in both worlds rather than becoming a true master of both. Those with a jay as a totem usually have a tremendous amount of ability, but it can be scattered or it is often not developed any more than is necessary to get by. It is not unusual to find individuals with blue jays as totems as being dabblers—especially in the psychic and metaphysical fields. True*

51

mastership requires dedication, responsibility, and committed development in all things in the physical and spiritual. The jay is a reminder to follow through on all things to not start something and leave it dangling.

The blue jay reflects that a greater time of resourcefulness and adaptability is about to unfold. You are going to have ample opportunities to develop and use your abilities.

The blue jay is actually a member of the crow family, and most crows have no fear. Crows and jays alike will gang up to harass and drive off owls and hawks. The jay is fearless and it is because of this, that it can help you connect with the deepest mysteries of the earth and the greatest of the heavens.[1]

I had been an untrained dabbler when I first got hold of the gift of empathy—or should I say it got hold of me? It was time for me to pick up the gift again and start where I left off. I would need to develop my intuition and emotional intelligence and learn to set boundaries, but this sign gave me the courage I needed to believe that the gift would not be used against me this time. That same day, I was in the parking lot putting some groceries in my car when I heard, "caw caw" above me. Glancing upward, I saw a huge black crow atop the light post next to my car.

While in this state of emotional upheaval, I did a radio interview with Lynn Serafinn in which I chatted about some ghost activity I had encountered in the past. After the interview, I marveled at how effective the protection measures I had been using really were. I hadn't been bothered by ghosts or the energy of others for quite some time. When I got the jaybird message, I told the universe I was ready to stop dabbling with my psychic gifts and get serious about developing them in order to help bring heaven to earth. That's when I got a letter in the mail. It was my next confirmation or sign that it was time to move forward. Remember Jerry and his message about Mason? Dianne's letter reached me at the perfect time due to the message Spirit gave me about the blue jay. Mason was a friend of Jerry's, who worked at the Kroger where he died. Jerry had visited with Mason just minutes before he walked outside and was killed in the parking lot. She was the last person (who actually knew him) to see him alive. More than likely, Jerry's spirit was hanging around her after the sudden death of his body.

I learned of Dr. Caron Goode when I wrote some articles for her intuitive parenting blog when I first started my writing business. We "met" a second time when we were both guest panelists on Spirit Author's Grand Opening Week. Shortly thereafter, she asked me to endorse her book, *Kids Who See Ghosts, Guide Them Through Their Fear.* In return for her sending me a copy of her book, I sent her a copy of my book, *The Sid Series ~ A Collection of Holistic Stories for Children.* She loved it so much she gave it a wonderful review on Amazon and asked for my book on death and afterlife.

Caron and I were soon again joined in a book launch for *Awakened Wisdom* by Patrick Ryan. We began a Facebook page to combine our information about intuitive children, ghosts, and other spiritual topics. One morning, before a scheduled phone meeting with Caron to discuss our next venture, I was sitting in my meditation spot. I glanced at the clock and noted the time was 9:05 a.m. Doreen Virtue's book, *Angel*

Numbers 101 was on the table next to me, so I picked it up and found 905. It read: "God is guiding you to make a healthful and positive change in your career so that you can devote your time and energy toward your Divine life purpose."

During this time, a male cardinal had been intentionally flying into the windows on the east and south sides of my house for over a month. Not only it is annoying to be awakened at sunrise by the nonstop body slamming, but it seems he would have a tremendous headache or a broken neck and would give up. I learned that male cardinals are territorial and that he was probably seeing his reflection in the glass and attacking what he thinks is another male cardinal infringing upon his territory. This activity began during a time when I was working on a project that had a very short deadline. The more I tried to move toward the finish line, the less I seemed to get accomplished. Seeing the similarities between my activity and that of this kamikaze bird, I figured the cardinal had a message for me, so I looked up cardinal totem in *Animal Speak.* Here's what I found:

> *. . . Unlike many other birds, cardinals are year-round residents and their influence and the archetypal energies associated with them can be accessed all year long. They remind us that regardless of the time of day or year, we always have opportunity to renew our own vitality and recognize the importance of our own life roles.*
>
> *These birds are named for the cardinals of the Roman Catholic Church, with their bright red robes. If it is your totem, it may reflect past-life connections with the church, or even a*

*reviving of more traditional religious beliefs,
regardless of denomination.*[2]

I memorized a lot of Bible verses in my early years, and
now that the cardinal was in my life, I was also hearing
verses of scripture in my head. Kind of like the song
you can't stop singing. I wondered what was up with
that.

Another confirmation came from the Goddess Wisdom
Titles app on my iPhone. Here is a
summary/paraphrase of the material on pp 32-35:

> *To understand Divine power, you must absorb
> and study the sacred texts of your own society
> and then include them and go beyond their
> interpretations in order to begin to know a
> higher code of conduct. Try on many points of
> view other than just those taught you as a
> child. Integrate many points of view from
> different cultures. Every perspective has
> something to offer and is an important part of
> the whole.*[3]

It was all beginning to make sense. For years, I tried to
use my intuitive and healing gifts in the church. When I
would attempt to relate dreams and visions I was
having about the organization's future, I was rejected
by the clergy. Did I really need a cardinal attacking my
window to remind me that a prophetess is not welcome
in her home church? Spirit was saying to let go of the
hateful thoughts I had held toward the system and all
its fear-based manipulative efforts to control people. I
had to forgive the church in order to move on.

It sure helped to have confirmation during this
transition—especially when it involved reopening to a
gift that had caused me so much distress in the past—

but the awakening of this gift came very quickly. Through this intuitive guidance I revived my blog, We Are One in Spirit (http://weareoneinspirit.blogspot.com), and started a podcast about being one with our creator. I had initiated the blog and podcast in 2006 and put them on the back burner while I propelled my business forward. Within a week's time after restarting the podcast I had guests lined up for months in advance. The next thing I knew, I was writing this book.

Signs like these come to all of us. We simply have to be attuned to recognize them.

Sources for Chapter 4:

1. Andrews, Ted. <u>Animal Speak</u>. Llewellyn Publications, Woodbury, Minnesota, 2009, page 121-122

2. Andrews, Ted. Animal Speak. Llewellyn Publications, Woodbury, Minnesota, 2009, page 124-125

3. Wells, Pamela. Goddess Wisdom Titles app for iPhone. "Emperor." p 32. Artmagic Publishing, 2009. <http://www.wisdomtitles.com>.

Chapter 5 ~ Stories from Other Empaths

Empaths can pick up other peoples' emotions when least expected. For example, if someone at work had an argument on the way to work, and then walks over to you and starts a conversation, you might feel the energy of his residual anger. This can be very confusing if you are not aware of his previous phone call. You may actually feel angry and think it is your stuff. If you suddenly feel angry for no reason or start complaining about something that you care virtually nothing about, you have probably picked up on the emotions of someone around you. This type of "mirroring," which seems to be more prevalent when we are exhausted or stressed out, can cause an empathic person to behave in an irrational manner.

In this chapter I will include excerpts from interviews I did with empaths while researching and writing this book. You will find a wide variety of situations in which folks have found themselves as a result of this intuitive gift. Some of these people have just realized they are empaths; others are veteran empaths who are using this intuitive gift as part of their healing practice.

Intuitive information is largely received and stored in your unconscious mind where you may not be aware of it.

Empathic abilities can be both a gift and a curse. One person I interviewed said that it has both saved his life and broken his heart. "I thought I was an agoraphobic for the longest because when I was around a lot of people I felt overwhelmed," said Jonathan. "I thought it was anxiety, but then I began to be able to tell when someone was lying to me. It can hurt to know someone you love is lying to you."

Gregg Braden's book, *The Spontaneous Healing of Belief, Shattering the Paradigm of False Limits* goes into detail about how our emotions, thoughts, feelings, and beliefs affect every aspect of our lives. He writes:

> *Emotion is the power that drives us forward in life. Love or fear is the driving force that propels us through the walls of resistance and catapults us beyond the barriers that keep us from our goals, dreams, and desires. Just as the power of any engine needs to be harnessed for it to be useful, the power of emotion must be channeled and focused for it to serve us in our lives.*[1]

One empath I interviewed told about being in San Francisco where he and a friend had been doing acid and were coming down. His friend was in the bathroom banging his head on the pipe and having a bad trip. The empath was in the other room when suddenly he started screaming. He was feeling his friend's physical pain. Doing drugs is a very bad idea for anyone, much less someone who is an empath. Besides the damage they do to the physical body, drugs cause an energy-sensitive person to become even more vulnerable to psychic attacks. Many drugs (including prescription ones) and overuse of alcohol can lower your vibrational level. Mind-altering substances can send out a vibratory invitation to spirits who would like to prey off your energy. Empaths need to pay consistent attention to their energy field to sense when their boundaries are being violated. You are in no state to keep vigil while in a daze.

One person I heard from said she if she drove past a serious car accident, she would feel all the emotions that the people involved feel, including the confusion of the person who died. If there is someone in the car with her, she feels embarrassed about crying and having to answer their question, "Did you know someone in that accident?" and explain why she is crying.

Sandy, a mother of two boys, talked about experiencing severe emotional distress (able to feel everyone's emotions simultaneously and very strongly) since she was eight years old, and she said it keeps getting worse. Her grandmother, who was also empathic, died before she could teach Sandy how to manage the gift—actually, Sandy called it a curse that she never wanted. She couldn't go anywhere or be around people and she hated her life. Her two sons are also empathic and she doesn't want them to end up miserable. Sandy no longer recognizes her own feelings. This is so common among empaths that I am dedicating an entire chapter to help you determine what it feels like to your own energy. Sandy also mentioned that the only way she knew to turn off the emotion was to be cold and unloving. This is a temptation to many empathic people, but because we are so loving, it really goes against our grain to treat people unkindly or shut them out of our heart. While we seem to do better living alone, we also have a desire to help others and have close relationships. There is a way to remain open without being unloving—it's called detachment and we will explore this later on.

Gloria Mitchell's parents took her to see *Bambi* at the theater when she was under the age of five years. Bambi's mother was killed in the beginning, which really upset her. For the rest of the movie Gloria kept asking, "Where's the mommy?" I think we all cried during that movie. I know I did and I was an adult watching it with my own kids! Gloria says the most painful example of empathy in her life concerns her parents. They lost their business a few years ago, and for three years lived in a horrible house and had virtually no social life. There was a palpable sadness—a terrible energy—floating around the house. Gloria visited them every other weekend and no matter how much she tried to go there with a positive attitude, she became depressed or angry within an hour of being around them. When she tried to talk to them about it they would brush it under the rug, but this proverbial elephant in the room only led to arguments. It wasn't just the house that was affected. This crappy energy was emanating from her parents, mostly her father, so whenever she took them to visit her brother in another state, the negativity poured off them. She always returned home feeling emotionally exhausted and depressed after being with them. The situation improved when her parents moved to a better house and started spending time with their friends. While things are by no means back to "normal" for them, Gloria feels a huge weight lifted from her.

Gloria's story reminds me to mention that places as well as people can hold energy from those who have lived there previously. If you enter a place and suddenly feel tense, uneasy, gloomy, or even frightened, or if you get physical sensations such as chills, gooseflesh, headache, or dizziness, you are likely picking up energies from what has transpired there. Because places and things absorb energy from the experiences they have "witnessed," empaths need extra protection in places like funeral homes, prisons, and crime scenes.

Ranoli is a holistic home inspector, home energy efficiency analyst, and real estate consultant whose mission is to help people heal their hearts and homes. She says that the thoughts and emotions of all who have ever been inside the house or walked on the land become part of the operating system for a property. Combine the earth energies with the electrical emissions from electrical power lines, cell phone towers, and antennas and you have a very powerful program working either against you or for you. Since empaths are sensitive to all types of energy, keeping your environment flowing with positive energy is very beneficial. Therefore, I have listed feng shui as one of the clearing exercises in Chapter 9 and have included Ranoli's contact information in the resources at the end of this book.

While writing this book, I visited a restaurant in a section of downtown that has a lot of negative energy. As I parked my car in the public garage I suddenly felt vulnerable. I was walking down the sidewalk when I felt the presence of two malicious thugs behind me. The energy was so strong and repulsive, I turned around to see if someone was following me. I saw no one. I knew my guides were protecting me and I didn't really feel afraid. I was simply aware. I thought no more about it as I met my husband for dinner.

On the way home, I had on the eyeglasses that I normally wear at my computer rather than the stronger prescription I need for nighttime driving. Plus, I experienced an unusual amount of traffic, my cell phone kept ringing, two people texted me, and one guy kept blowing his horn and flashing his lights at me. It wasn't until I pulled off the interstate at my exit that I realized I had been driving without my headlights on. Later that night when I went to bed, I felt angry and troubled. There had been a discrepancy about the bill and I thought I was still upset about that and my uneasy drive home. I let that energy go and felt better. However, I could not sleep because I kept sensing an unfamiliar presence. As I looked around my bedroom that moonlit night, I saw a dark cloud moving across the room. I didn't feel concerned and only half believed there was really anything there. As I often do when I'm trying to fall asleep, I began meditating to help my body relax. My mind was racing, but I finally slept, only to awake at sunrise still feeling aggravated. I didn't want to get up after only having five hours of sleep. So, I rolled over and dozed off. When I got up an hour or so later I still felt perturbed. "What's up with this?" I finally asked my guides. "You might want to do something about the entity you brought home last night." It all made sense—the eerie presence near the parking garage, the crazy drive home, the aggravation. I immediately lit a sage bundle and smudged myself and my house and my car. That took care of the problem.

One drawback to being empathetic is that it can make you afraid of connecting closely with others because you feel too much of their stuff. You can't avoid being in the energy field of the person with whom you are physically intimate. I have to constantly remind myself that my husband's energy is not my energy and that I don't have to solve his problems, or try to fix him, or change his moods. That's a bad habit I'm still trying to break. Empaths naturally want to make people happy and most of us tend to be caretakers. It takes a conscious effort to let people be who and how they are without allowing their energy to bring us down. It takes practice in trusting and developing your relationship with yourself and understanding how to work with your emotions in a helpful way.

Samantha says being an empath is generally draining. "You may feel dread or have to prepare yourself to be around people. It makes it impossible to get down to what *you* truly feel instead of what others are projecting to you," says Samantha. "There are a few people who are very good at disguise. Their energy may feel positive at first, but they can't keep up the wall very long."

Empaths need a place each day where they can be alone to replenish their positive energy. For that reason, living alone is essential for Samantha. She says this is the only way she can begin her day without feeling anxious or sometimes deeply depressed. On the contrary, animals calm her because they present themselves honestly and are pure beings at all times. "I don't usually feel much from them unless they have been abused or are hurt," she says. "Sometimes I feel the same around very young children."

Bridgette developed the gift of intuition as a child growing up with a bi-polar mother. She never knew what her mom's mood would be from one minute to the next, so she tuned into her mom's energy field to avoid constant verbal and mental abuse. She doesn't like tapping in now and wishes she didn't have the ability to feel what other people feel because it drains her and makes her feel depressed and terrible. "Have you ever seen a dog that winces when someone tries to pet it? That is me, figuratively, every time I have to be around people," she says. "I hate being out in public at all. If I make eye contact with anyone, I feel uncomfortable because I get a sense from them that I don't want."

Julie Isaac says she has always known that she picked up people's emotional energy, but she didn't know she was picking up their aches and pains, as well.

> *"For years I thought I was a hypochondriac until one Thursday night when I knew with every fiber of my being that I was going to have a heart attack. Going to have! There was no pain, so there was no reason to go to the hospital to tell them that I would soon be having a heart attack. I decided to watch TV and relax until I felt something that would tell me it's time to go to the hospital. Then, in an instant, the feeling/knowing lifted. It was so bizarre. The next day, Friday, I went to work and my boss was out sick. On Monday, they told us that she had had a heart attack on Thursday night. That's when I realized I wasn't a hypochondriac; I was picking up on other people's physical energy."*

How Empathy is Used for Good

Tom Goode "feels" people's pain, sees and senses the patterns empathically, and does his healing work using these senses. He first discovered he was an empath when he began a sales career and could tell when a person was going to buy and when they were not. He says that empathy is no more or less a gift than being able to play baseball, though clearly some people are better at it than others. Tom says that most people are out of their bodies, so numb to its feelings and so unfamiliar with how they themselves feel that they cannot differentiate their own energy from the energy of others.

Being empathetic is useful to Tom because it allows him to know the truth or falsity in situations and people. As he became more sensitive, a trait that can be cultivated, he began to use empathy to assist others. If you were to call him and ask for facilitation in finding an answer to a problem area in your life, dissolving a pain, or correcting an energetic imbalance, he would "read" your energy and the emotion/thought behind it to assist you in finding your own answers. He says, "It saves you, as a client, much time and money for me to be able to do this by telephone, rather than have you come to an office or other physical location." Empathy is useful in correcting symptoms of imbalance in animals as well.

Hillary Raimo is the founder and author of the signature UNtraining™ series. As an empath she feels energy and can tune in to the emotional energy of another person, animal, or event in order to read it. She says the gift can often be dismissed by others or mistaken for psychological issues. (I'm sure people who saw me praying thought I was crazy!) Hillary pursued psychology in college so she could better understand herself, but when she began to explore shamanistic and psychic studies it clicked that she had been empathic all her life. She now uses this gift in her work as an intuitive healer.

"Empathy is a gift we all have," says Hillary. "It is part of who we are biologically. We are an intuitive and psychic species. Our psychic senses have been dulled down for many reasons, and dismissed. But when we reconnect with that ability within us it reconnects us to our natural state of divinity. A oneness that plugs us back into nature and the cosmos."

Gini Grey is a transformational coach who reads energy and teaches others to do the same. She studied spiritual awareness, energy healing, and aura reading for several years. By learning to create healthy energy boundaries, differentiating her energy from others' energy, and clearing her field, she was able to start reading energy using clairvoyance (sixth chakra aspect) instead of feeling energy through clairsentience (aspect of the second chakra). This allowed her to stop taking on others' problems, emotions, pain etc. She writes about empathy and intuition in her articles and books (www.ginigrey.com/wp). She has graciously given me permission to use excerpts of her material throughout this book.

Sources for Chapter 5:

Braden, Gregg. The Spontaneous Healing of Belief, Shattering the Paradigm of False Limits. Hay House, 2008. Page 65.

Chapter 6 ~ Empathetic Children and Teens

Empathy is what makes other people matter to us and reminds us to acknowledge the people around us as we understand and share their feelings. At what stage in our social development does empathy begin?

As an intuitive counselor, Dr. Caron Goode is an expert on the early development of empathy and a child's sensitivity to others. She notes that empathy exists in early mother-infant bonding. Even before birth, a baby in the womb is sensitive to the mother's feelings, whether positive, neutral, or negative. Once born, a baby shows receptivity to both parents' anger, tension, and depression, as well as their caring, responsiveness, and love.

In an article titled "Empathy: Big Feelings from Little Ones,"[1] the Talaris Research Institute concludes that life starts with a biological bent toward empathy. From birth, babies have the ability to respond to the emotions of others. You've probably noticed how they imitate your facial expressions, smiling in response to your smile. They also may cry if they hear another baby cry. This type of response is a step in the development of empathy and the ability to share the feelings of another person.

Martin Hoffman, a psychology professor at New York
University who did the first studies on infant empathy
in the 1970s, questioned why babies cry when they hear
another baby crying. Does this mean that the baby is
truly concerned for his fellow human, or just annoyed
by the noise? A study built on Hoffman's work was
conducted in Italy in which researchers played for
infants a recording of other babies crying. As predicted,
the tears started flowing. But the odd thing is that when
researchers played babies a recording of their own
cries, they rarely cried. This shows that there is some
rudimentary form of empathy in place, right from birth,
but Hoffman also noted that the emotion tends to fade
over time. Babies older than six months no longer cry
when they hear another baby crying, but they may
grimace when they notice the discomfort of others.

In August 2005, the society section of *Newsweek* ran
an article titled "Reading Your Baby's Mind" by Martha
Brant and Pat Winger. An experiment was conducted
with a mother and child in the Human Sciences lab at
Texas Tech University. The six-month-old girl was
placed in a high chair while her mother was given a
children's book and asked to engage in a conversation
with Sybil Hart, an associate professor of human
development and the leader of the study. Hart and the
mother talked about the book without paying any
attention to the baby. As the two women chatted, the
baby showed no emotional response. Sybil then placed
a lifelike baby doll in the mother's arms and instructed
her to cuddle and talk to the doll while continuing to
ignore her daughter. The baby's response began with a
smile, then she kicked her high chair in an attempt to
get her mother's attention. When the mother paid her
no attention, the baby started screaming and crying.
Sybil took the doll and allowed the mother to comfort

her child. Ms. Hart repeated the scenario hundreds of times, and in nearly every case the babies responded with jealousy.

I've witnessed a similar response with my two grandsons, who were born two weeks apart in 2009. At the writing of this book, Jonas is sixteen and a half months and Liam is seventeen months old. Even though their personalities are totally different, the boys play well together. But already they are showing signs of jealousy. If I hold one, I have to hold the other one *at the same time*, which is not easy. Holding two 25-pound bundles of wiggling joy causes me to have to sit down. If one has a toy the other one wants, he will grab it right out of his cousin's hand. If I give one boy a snack or juice, the other one wants a snack and juice. I could not play favorites even if I wanted to. I was really surprised when I found them showing jealousy at such an early age in their moral and social development. That made me wonder if they were able to show empathy. My answer came quickly.

The boys had only been walking a couple of months and were still a little unsteady on their feet. They were hugging each other when Jonas fell backward and bumped his head on the wall. Liam squatted down next to him as if to see if his cousin was okay. I was amazed! He really seemed to care that Jonas fell down. Who knows? Maybe he was just checking to make sure he didn't have an extra Goldfish clinched in his sticky little fist. I did some research about this and found that, according to Dr. Kyle Pruett, children's brains develop empathy from birth to age eight years. I witnessed this with Jonas one Sunday. He was excitedly flinging his arms while his mom was feeding him. He accidentally hit his mom in the face. When she jumped back and said, "Ouch!". Jonas hung his head down as if he was sorry for his action.

The article by the Talaris Research Institute[1] also mentioned a study about how empathy develops. The study was conducted with children in three age ranges: 13–15 months old, 18–20 months old, and 23–25 months old. The researchers trained mothers to observe their children's responses to the emotions of others. Researchers visited once a month to observe and videotape the children. The study found that more than half of the babies aged 13–15 months not only responded to the emotion they saw, but they made an attempt to help the other person feel better by hugging, patting, or touching another person who was showing distress. More than half of those aged 18–20 months showed an increase in this type of behavior, and responded with touch as well as verbal responses such as asking if the saddened person was okay. Some offered food or a blanket to comfort the distressed person. All but one of the children aged 23–25 months showed concern and a desire to help others (even a stranger) without the encouragement of a parent or caregiver. Not all the children showed concern or empathy for others. Some even laughed when they caused distress for another person. This leads me to believe that the gift of empathy is not something all children continue to develop as they age. However, empathic children become empathic teens and adults. Jonas' brother, Sidney, is almost ten years old. I'm forever impressed with the love, respect, and concern he shows his baby brother as they play together.

Babies absorb the mental and emotional energy of the people around them. They don't filter anything; they simply receive. An empathic child easily picks up on the emotions, energy, or thoughts of others. The Latin word for emotion is *emovere*, which means movement. Suppressing an emotion prevents the natural movement of vital energy. As Karol Truman says in her book by the same title, "feelings buried alive never die." Denying and resisting what you feel only makes things worse. The repressed emotion is stored in our cells and will demand to be dealt with at a later time. When a child stuffs his or her feelings it creates an inward vortex of spiraling emotions that can continue to pull the child downward for years to come. If your child has bouts of depression, notice what triggers are associated with the episodes. Who has he/she been around? What activity is he/she about to embark upon? Is the child getting visual images, having dreams, or sensing something isn't quite right? This intuitive insight could be a clue to a past life issue that needs to be healed or an indication that he or she is involved in something that is not in alignment with the soul's higher purpose. You can help redirect the child or teen by listening and offering to help them end their unhealthy relationship or association with a person or organization. And if you see that your energy-sensitive child is showing distress from having the gift of empathy, teach him or her how to do the exercises in Chapter 9.

Intuitive children and teens know their personal truth. Any distortion of that truth can cause them to feel confused, depressed, unbalanced, or even sick. Childhood depression can be carried into adulthood if it is not dealt with when it first appears. When I was a teenager, I felt depressed every weekend. Without fail sometime near dusk each Saturday night, I would feel a sense of foreboding sadness that I could not explain. I simply learned to live with it.

Before I began writing this book, I encountered a time period when I felt angry and depressed and wasn't sure why. I knew I was picking up on someone else's energy, so I cleared my field. That brought some relief but I sensed that something was coming up for healing. I was pretty sure the remaining energy was my stuff because the feeling reminded me so much of how I felt as a teen. Sometimes when we are in the middle of a situation, it's hard to see the big picture, so I asked Caron for help. Without prior knowledge of what was going on in my life, she asked for permission to access and read my energy. Permission granted, she got an image in which she saw a dust bowl blowing up a storm around me. Intuitive children and adults are able to get visual pictures like this—much like a dream while being awake. These visions are the soul's message and provide clues as to what is going on at a deeper level. If you have a child who gets mental pictures, try to help him or her put the clues together and find out what is coming up for healing.

The cloud was so thick, it obscured all visibility. Caron saw a baby tied to my back but the baby was dead—it was either stillborn or died shortly after birth. I was alone in the wilderness, separated from everyone I knew and loved. I was trying to find my way back home and help everyone else get home safely in the process. This vision seemed to be a past life—perhaps I really lived somewhere out west in another lifetime—but since there really is no such thing as linear time when it comes to soul development, Caron and I both knew my soul was trying to give me a message.

I quickly made a connection with the symbolism of Caron's vision. I had linked up in a joint venture partnership with a wonderful gentleman who professed to be relaxed in his Christian beliefs. But as we continued to work together on business-related projects, it became apparent that he was much stauncher in his religious beliefs than he originally professed. The unspoken confrontation inside me was going against everything that I had come to stand for, and my soul was stirring up the emotion of anger to get me to leave the business venture with this man. He wanted the business to be based on his religious beliefs, which excluded my interviewing guests who presented any other ideology. While I was being tolerant outwardly, I was raging inwardly—not at my business partner, but at myself because I was stifling my own voice, as I had as a child—in an effort to move this business venture forward.

The wilderness represented the years I had gone along with the group of people (family, friends, church fellowship) with whom I had felt a sense of community. When I broke away from the pack, I felt all alone and was carrying a tremendous burden on my back. The message of oneness with God/Goddess (rather than separation from our Creator, which my religion taught me) is the message I am to bring to the Earth. Sharing this message makes me feel at home. I want everyone to find a way back home to his or her own divinity. The dead baby in Caron's vision was my current business venture that could not live or grow in the confines of the doctrine that my partner insisted upon bringing into our business venture. No matter how much I loved my religious friend and the idea of sharing my message with the world, I could not remain in the partnership because it meant repressing my authentic self and going along with the fundamentalist doctrine that teaches people that they are sinners bound for hell and damnation because they are separated from an angry

God and in need of a blood sacrifice for reconciliation. I cannot support this belief in a punishing God that treats his children worse than the most abusive human parent.

Caron and I visualized removing the baby from my back, thanked it for the gift it had brought, and released my grief over losing the business opportunity. This vision represented a lifelong theme for me. Whether it was a glimpse into a past life or a message given in symbols, the information I gained from our session showed me that the key contributor to the depression I experienced as a teenager and the anger I was currently dealing with were an intuitive message from my soul. We are here to live an authentic life—not to make everyone happy at our own expense.

Little did I know that my business partner was also very uncomfortable with my "oneness" message. The day after my clearing session with Caron, he called to say he could not continue in our business venture because our beliefs were at opposite ends of the pole. Both of us were compromising what we believed in.

Empathy and intuition give us the ability to better understand how we are connected to other living things. It is a form of communication with others, nature, animals, and even higher or spirit forms of life. I think we are all born with empathic ability, but most of us shut the sensing ability down at some point, like I did, because it causes such discomfort and overload. By shutting down, we live in our heads and are pretty much out of touch with our body and our own emotions.

Being an "unaware" empath is very draining for an adult. Just imagine what it feels like to be an intuitive kid and not have the language to explain it to your parents. A child who sees or hears in the spirit realm may act out because he or she feels overwhelmed and does not know how to express what he or she is experiencing. The problem is compounded when adults will not listen, try to hush the child, or refuse to believe the child's report of psychic incidents.

When Iris was thirteen, her dad planned a fishing trip with the family. As much as she loved fishing, that sunny July morning was quite upsetting for her. She had not slept well the previous night and when she awoke she felt uncomfortable, nauseated, and like there was a magnetic force discouraging her from going on the trip. As the rest of the family happily approached the van, Iris begged her dad to please reschedule the trip. She told him that she felt sick and scared and that they shouldn't go. Confused by her behavior, he commanded her to get in the van.

When they arrived at the lake, the clan spread out along the banks with no more than twelve feet between them—that was the family fishing rule. Inwardly, Iris was still freaking out and disturbed but she kept quiet as she took her fishing pole and sat on a rock.

Two minutes later, her little sister came to sit next to her and asked, "What's wrong? Why didn't you want to come on the trip?"

Suddenly, Iris heard a distant, shattered voice yelling, "Help me!"

"Shhhh!" Iris said to her sister. "Listen. Did you hear that?"

Her sister didn't hear zip and looked at Iris like she was crazy.

As she kept hearing the same words, Iris noticed the voice was coming from the other side of the lake. The voice sounded like a flute, not like a human voice. Then she realized it was coming out of the water. Iris ran to her dad and told him that she heard voices from the other side of the lake.

"There is no one at the other side of the lake. It's closed to the public. Go take a nap. You're in my fishing spot."

At this point Iris thought she was going crazy! But she went back to her spot and started drawing. A half hour later, she heard her family members crying and yelling, "We lost him!"

Danny, her 16-year-old cousin, decided to sneak off to catch the larger fish where the boats go. Danny had won awards for being the best swimmer and fisher, yet he drowned that day.

Iris' dad warned her to never tell these stories to anyone because it might lead them astray from the Christian faith. Now that her dad is gone, she feels free to tell her stories—and there are many.

Iris has precognizant, clairaudient, and clairsentient gifts at work in her life. The precognizant magnetic pull she felt was for the purpose of getting her attention in order to have her dad cancel the trip or take extra precaution in knowing where each child was at all times. Hearing the voice crying for help is a clairaudient gift. The feeling of nausea is a clairsentient ability. Many empathic healers use this gift to ascertain where in the body their patients need a healing flow of energy directed.

These gifts are just as common and useful as gifts of music, art, teaching, or other talents humans possess, but it's not typical for families to discuss paranormal experiences that do not align with their religious doctrine or are frowned upon by the church. It's probably not a good idea to go to church on Sunday and admit that you see ghosts. However, had Iris' dad listened to her that day, Danny might still be in body today.

We do our intuitive children a great injustice when we invalidate their intuitive abilities. But, many parents simply don't know what to do with kids who see or hear spirits, predict future events, or know some family secret they haven't been told. In some cases, the "hushing" parent also has some paranormal gifts in operation that he or she is not comfortable talking about—maybe they were shushed by their parents and are simply passing down the advice they were given.

You may have heard of Indigo Children or Crystal Kids, who have intuitive gifts that surprise or even astound adults. These empathic children easily pick up on the feelings and thoughts of adults and others as they unconsciously reach into human and spirit energy fields to gather information and understand things around them. Seeing with their spiritual eyes, feeling with their spiritual senses, hearing with their spiritual ears, they may give information about a past life, tell of events before they happen, see ghosts, or know something about another person or situation that no one else does. Today, as many as one in four children have this ability and are tuned into the higher frequency all the time.

Because these children do not know how to set personal boundaries (or that they need to), they do not realize when they are in another person's mental or emotional space, much less how invasive this can be to that person. It can also affect the child's own vibrational level. As parents we need to teach our children how to properly use this empathic gift, but many adults do not trust their own intuition, much less recognize their children's spiritual abilities. Empathic kids and teens need someone they can talk to, and they need information on how to keep their auras clear and to open and shut their intuitive abilities at will. It is important for adults to help them learn how to do this and set energetic boundaries. The more you read and study this topic, the better you will be able to answer your children's questions. I hope you will relate to what you are learning here and help the children in your life develop their intuition.

In the next chapter, Dr. Caron Goode will share the four core temperaments as they relate to the psychological aspect of empathy.

Sources for Chapter 6:

1. "Empathy: big feelings from little ones." <u>Talaris Research Institute on Raising Children Network</u>. Accessed 18 November 2010. <http://ow.ly/3cN1M>.

Chapter 7 ~ Psychology of Empathy

Tenderness and kindness are not signs of weakness and despair, but manifestations of strength and resolution. ~ Kahlil Gibran

The Challenge of Empathy

The usually boisterous Meredith seemed subdued when she entered my office. Her posture sagged and she spoke in breathless tones.

"Welcome, come in. You sound very tired right now. Are you all right?"

"Caron, it seems like I've been trying to fight off this cold and sinus infection for months. So I am tired, but the reason I wanted to speak with you today was about an experience I had with Yelena, the woman I take care of."

"Sure, grab a cup of hot tea I made for you, and tell me about you and Yelena."

"Well, you know she is only seventy-two years old, but had an early onset of dementia, and I care for her. Within the last week, she has been inviting me into her garden. It's in her mind, not her yard, but she says that she likes to walk in the beautiful garden with roses and hedges. The words she uses paint a picture of an expansive English garden of a country estate. Well, I finally agreed to 'take a walk' in her garden. We sat together on her couch and held hands and closed our eyes. I asked her to describe everything to me, from every flower and its color to the fresh air she breathed.

"I felt like I stepped into her world of blue sky and fragrant honeysuckles. Even taking steps next to her was so real because her hand, which held mine, moved rhythmically against the couch between us. She was alive and vibrant in her world, and I felt this with her so vividly, that shifting back to sitting on the couch in her home was like being seated in an airplane that dropped from the sky and skidded to a sudden halt. I even felt nauseous."

"So, Meredith, is your feeling sick the concern? Or is it something about the mental journey with Yelena?" I asked.

"I was so connected to her that I felt everything she felt— the sense of freedom, the clear air, the sun warming my skin. I experienced her freedom somewhere in her mind, but I also experienced how her body felt, which was so tired, almost exhausted. I haven't been able to shake the exhausted feeling ever since."

"Are you are saying that still feeling tired a week later is connected to being tuned in to Yelena?"

"Definitely, and even a little dizziness sometimes. Have you ever heard of something like this? I mean, it is kind of weird, but my symptoms seem to be a direct result of the garden visit."

"Meredith," I explained, "I've heard what you describe called 'empathy fatigue.' This happens when a

caretaker, nurse, counselor, or anyone in the helping
professions takes on their client's symptoms. I have
heard other therapists' discussions at conferences
speaking of their personal symptoms after working
with clients who have stress-related illnesses.
Caretakers like you also experience fatigue in longer-
term situations. You have an empathic ability to know
your client's needs and that enables you to do your job
so well."

"You mean my ability to connect with and experience
my client's feelings makes me vulnerable?"

"Yes, that is what I mean. Your strength then is also
your challenge."

Core Temperaments and Empathy

> *The great gift of human beings is that we have
> the power of empathy, we can all sense a
> mysterious connection to each other. ~ Meryl
> Streep*

In the story above, Meredith, a trained nurse who chose
to leave a hospital setting and move into private care,
had the ability to resonate *with* another person on a
deep level. Such resonance is achieved through
empathy, the ability to feel *with* her client, not to feel
for them or *about* them. Resonating with her clients is
a striking intuitive knowing, which enables her to
predict their needs and provide an unprecedented
quality of care.

The ability to resonate with others is the character
strength of a person whose core temperament is
Interpersonal. Other strengths of a Interpersonal core
temperament are adaptability and being supportive.
The Interpersonal style is one of the Four Basic Core

Temperaments—the other three are called Behavioral, Cognitive, and Affective—identified here from the research and writing of Terry Anderson, PhD, the founder of Consulting Resource Group International and author of more than a dozen assessments, training and development tools, and books.

Over the last two decades, the science of temperaments and research on how people think has validated that each person is born with a core temperament, which is nature's approximate 20 percent genetic contribution to one's overall personality. Our environments contribute the other 80 percent by virtue of our ability to adapt.

Four Basic Core Temperaments provide the cornerstones for people's interactive preferences, how they learn, and what motivates them. From the table below, you see that persons with Interpersonal and Affective styles relate well to people. While persons with a Cognitive style are immersed in information or data, they relate well to people as team members and partners because they are sensitive to feelings of others. The Behavioral style person is internally motivated by personal goals and achievements and may be the least sensitive to other people's feelings.

The chart on the next page shows the Four Basic Core Temperaments and how each interacts, learns, and is motivated.

	Behavioral	Cognitive	Interpersonal	Affective
Interacts best with	Tasks and achievement	Data and analysis	People through supporting	People and creative activities
Learns best through	Personal, hands-on experience	Visual processing	Auditory processing	Feeling and intuition
Motivated by	Challenge, competition, achievement	Analysis, theory, research, discovery	Helping, service, and connection	Networking, creativity, fun

So, if science tells us that all children are born with the capacity for empathy, what happens as we mature and our core temperaments adapt to our environments? Might we as adults lose that ability to connect and feel?

Empathy is more than feeling pain; it is also connecting to another's struggle or emotional intention as well as feelings of joy and celebration. Babies demonstrate empathy in a global sense. If other babies cry, then babies respond with crying. By the time a child is two and a half years old, he or she has developed a self-identity and understands the feelings of distress belonging to his playmate or parent or sibling. You will see preschool children empathize by reaching out to alleviate another's distress through words or touch. By age eight, a child understands the human plight of birth, death, and vulnerability.

Children depend upon the demonstrations of responsiveness, warmth, and empathy from the people in their world to continue cultivating connection and empathy within themselves. Otherwise, their ability to remain empathic is up for grabs. Assuming empathy continues to develop, then how do adults of different styles show empathy?

- While people with Behavioral styles are doers and high achievers, their ability to be empathic is shown through "doing" compassionate acts. Their empathy might be modeled on doing nice things or giving gifts.

- Cognitive people prefer to work with information, data, research, and theoretical models; yet they are very sensitive to how others feel, and their intuitive radar senses changes in the emotional atmosphere of their environments. They feel safe being empathic in more intimate situations, like with partners or close friends. They wouldn't be the type of people to intrude on another's personal space, or wish another to intrude in their space.

- Those with Interpersonal styles are excellent listeners, thrive on providing service, instructions, and support, and they easily adapt to changing circumstances.

- Those who have an Affective style are intuitive and also feel other people deeply. They are often happy to assist others.

Empathy Isn't Touchy-Feely Anymore

At a basic level, empathy is being attuned to another's emotions and intentions. The next level of empathy involves taking action to help another, whether alleviating fears and pain or supporting or celebrating someone. More complex forms of empathy occur when people join together for survival of struggles or to pursue the vision fueled by emotional connectedness. These show us how capable we are of making deep connections. The explanation for these connections comes with the discovery of "mirror neurons."

At the University of Parma, Italy, researchers found that when macaque monkeys observe another monkey or human perform an action like cracking a nut, the neurons that fire when the monkey itself performs the action also fires in response to watching another individual. Mirror neurons create a neuro-physiological link between one's own experience and that of another individual. Several studies confirm that when humans observe another person's intentional action and/or emotional expressions, they activate brain areas that are also engaged when the person would perform the action or experience the emotion himself.

This neuro-imaging research changes the way we view ourselves and also what we value. When we are not responded to, we feel unappreciated, lonely, or withdrawn. To feel loved, whole, appreciated, and useful, we must be in a relationship where empathy connects us. We now understand that we are hard-wired to resonate with each other at profound levels, thus driving our desires to belong and for bonding, connection, companionship, and affection. We are hardwired for empathy, and we share this trait with apes and other mammals.

The Empathy Process

We can describe empathy as a process of observing another's state—mental, emotional, and physical—which leads to specific brain centers' activations in the observer. As Yvonne describes throughout this book, empathy is closely aligned with one's intuition, in that empathy clearly provides the closest we might come to "knowing" another person—feeling their pain and joys, a communing of kindred spirits. All types of empathy can be a source of insight.

Once a perceiver's empathy is activated, their responses could be one or any combination of the following:

- Cognitive – I think. Leading with data, analysis information – expressing intuition through ideas and concepts.

- Behavioral – I do good deeds. I achieve inner satisfaction in this way.

- Affective – I feel you. Leading with a sixth sense of intuition, knowing something to be true and aware of energy boundaries.

- Interpersonal – How can I serve you? I feel deeply attuned to other's moods and experience intuition through feelings and emotional sensing.

To enhance empathy and work with another, these strategies will help.

- Visualization, seeing internally, plays an important role in the empathic process and heightens the physiology of feeling.

- Mimicry or imitation of another's words or actions allows one to have a better sense of what the other intends and expresses.

- Practicing attuning to another through modeling and role-playing enhances an understanding of another person and his or her environment. Like walking in another's shoes, you would understand the context of another's situation.

A Case for Empathy

Sarah was a forty-two-year-old mom of two teenage sons and the wife of a banking executive. Returning home from a meeting at her local Catholic church on a snowy December evening, her car struck an icy patch and spun out of control, off the road, and into a thick, broad oak tree. When her neighbor, who was also traveling home, saw the incident, he called for help and then informed Sarah's family. Sarah's family met her at the hospital emergency room, waited through tests, and learned that she suffered a severe concussion. Sarah could expect headaches, some short-term memory loss, and fatigue.

What Sarah shared with no one was that after she hit her head and blacked out for an undetermined length of time, she was enthralled in an intense conversation with Jesus, who was seated before her in radiant light. She felt herself to be in another realm, where she heard his words in her head, like telepathy, and she heard herself ask Him questions. Her experience, through which she felt uplifted and joyous, was very real to her, and she remembered it vividly. In fact the image of Jesus seemed fried into her brain, as she could hear him and see him. The event dramatically changed Sarah's perception.

She kept the changes to herself until she had a strange lunch one day with her husband, Gregg. They spoke of how well she was recovering. She lifted her head while chewing a bite of roast beef, looked into his eyes and nodded to him in agreement about taking a vacation. She took his hand and was struck by a knowing that her husband's heart attack was imminent. Frightened, she blurted out, "I am feeling your heart, and it feels sick."

"You know I don't have heart problems, Sarah. Do you think this is part of the concussion's symptoms?" Sarah confessed that she since the "accident," she had felt a dark cloudiness in the lungs of an asthmatic neighbor child, and had several other experiences involving sickness in people. She told Gregg that while this frightened her a little, she was more intrigued that this might be a gift coming to light, perhaps a new way to help people.

Sarah thought Gregg would listen, be supportive and explore the possibility of this new feeling. When she saw how horrified he was, she knew she would never be able to tell him about her Jesus experience. He immediately whipped out his mobile phone and scheduled a psychiatric consultation for her. The psychiatrist suggested medication to stop hallucinations, and planned continued appointments to look for any further difficulties caused by the concussion. Sarah tossed the prescription in the trash, and found another psychiatrist, who spoke to her of interventions without medication.

After listening to her story, the second psychiatrist explained to Sarah about a new diagnostic category for religious or spiritual experiences listed in the *Diagnostic and Statistical Manual-4th Edition*, which offers the ability for treatment without making her experience a pathology or part of a disease.

"Sarah," the doctor said, "it sounds like you may not have Gregg's support for this, but I would describe this as a spiritual experience, and I think you should learn to work with this new talent, like a latent empathy now blooming. Why not approach this new experience as not mystical, but more scientifically. See if it fades away as the concussion heals. First, start journaling the voice in your head. Connection to an inner wisdom is a positive thing, but we don't know yet how this inner wisdom guides you or what it shares with you. Explore and write down the feelings you get about friends and neighbors, and then follow up in conversation to see how accurate your perceptions are. Train your empathy and see where it leads you. Only time will tell you if the result is positive or if it leads to anxiety and disruption from trauma and a medical condition."

Empathy Has Been Around, Just Not Practiced

The empathy shown to Sarah by her second psychotherapist was a perfect modeling for her of a nonjudgmental approach to her own experiences, especially in the light of her husband feeling Sarah should medicate her symptoms. The modeling of empathy in therapies is not new; it has been around awhile, but mostly forgotten.

Most empathic persons in the helping professions view Carl Rogers as the strongest promoter of empathy, as described in his book, *A Way of Being*. On page 142 he states, "An empathic way of being with another person has several facets. It means entering the private perceptual world of the other . . . . It means temporarily living in the other's life, moving about in it delicately without making judgments; it means sensing meanings of which he or she is scarcely aware . . . It includes communicating your sensings of the person's world . . . frequently checking with the person as to the accuracy of your sensings."[1]

While Roger's emphasis was on the therapeutic relationship, his influence remains a steadfast focus in therapeutic communities. Yet, an integral (more complete) model of empathy by Arthur J Clark, was presented in the *Journal of Counseling & Development* and suggested that "When attempting to empathically understand a client, the counselor fleetingly engages in processes involving identification, imagination, intuition, and felt-level experiencing. In a sense, a counselor's self becomes a tool for empathic understanding and forming hypotheses in an immediate counseling context."[2]

The acceptance of intuition, use of imagination, and identifying with the client's feeling at the visceral level might be more what an empathic person who needs to learn boundaries and emotional coping skills is seeking in a mental health practitioner. For example, a person seeking treatment for moodiness, the blues, or depression might not know that the latest and largest new study, which examined published and unpublished clinical trials for Prozac, Effexor, and Paxil found that antidepressants work no better than a placebo for most patients.[3] Prescription-writing folks do not serve empathic people whose depression or moodiness are associated with their interactive styles or core temperaments, their professions, or their sensitivity to others. Empaths are not typically clinically depressed due to biochemical origins.

Even mental health practitioners who carefully practice professional distancing are at risk for feeling drained and tired. A few I have known feel anxious and experience a client's issues when not "in session" at the office. As a result, empathy fatigue is fast becoming a more common discussion in many service professions like crisis volunteers, caregivers, nannies, nursing, rehabilitation specialists, teachers, social workers, and even parents who consistently care for a child with health or educational issues.

Profiling

If we were to follow the behavioral and scientific clues to profile an empath in today's world, the following characteristics apply:

Woman: Female brains have variations, which correlate with higher empathy levels than a male brain. The female in our society has greater investment in human evolution through her investiture in child bearing and involvement in child rearing.

Sensitive: Whether through unique variations in one's central nervous system, or learned through environmental trauma, an empath has low threshold levels for stimulation, whether it is lights, sounds, electro-magnetic frequencies, noise bombardment, or crowds.

Intuitive: Empaths usually process information through feeling, vicarious experiences, gut level hunches, or through proprioception. Feeling deeply can be confusing or creative, depending upon what the intuitive understands and the ability to appropriately express what is internal. They are adept in reading, sensing, and knowing other people.

Emotionality: Sometimes emotions may overwhelm an empath and be described in such metaphors as "I was having a great day until a dark cloud rained down sadness," or "The shopping was fun until I felt so heavy I had to sit down," or "I swing back and forth, just like a pendulum on a tall Grandfather's clock, between feeling great and feeling exhausted," or "People say I'm nuts because I feel everybody else's pain," or "I can't go to concerts because I *feel* everyone there."

To Nurture Peace and Balance

Like Sarah in the previous story, sensitive people with the profile of an empath may not be recognized as such in traditional therapy settings. An empathic person with enough savvy to know their gifts as a self-aware person still needs connection, and the best support comes from non-traditional health practitioners, who may themselves be intuitive, holistic, natural, or energy practitioners. These include transpersonal and spiritual healers and therapists, neurolinguistic (NLP) practitioners, specific types of energy healers, and massage therapists, full-wave breath trainers, rebirthers, and other breath workers, hypnotherapists, and Chinese medicine practitioners. Each group of individuals on this list works with the mind-body connection to create inner resonance.

Empaths would also find relief and focus in learning to accept, as well as pay attention to, the present moment. Cultivating awareness of presence is accomplished through meditation practices, and also through exercises called mindfulness strategies. The benefits of such practices is to see clearly the mental habits that create suffering, pain, anxiety, or fear—some of the emotions that empaths feel with and around other people with these emotions.

Practicing mindfulness can be as simple as watching something in nature that brings you to the here and now: colorful flowers, passing clouds, a glowing moon, a gathering thunderstorm, or lightning on the horizon. Listening to music redirects unfocused consciousness to an uplifting melody. Transforming irritating emotional energies into vacuuming, decluttering the closet, or arranging flowers is a positive practice. Mindfulness doesn't take time, but it does take a willingness to shift your attention, take a deep breath and relax a moment, or take a walk and enjoy yourself.

As empaths, our journey may be to embrace, feel, and connect, but also to thrive, celebrate, and deepen awareness, not only for ourselves, but also for others with whom we are connected.

Sources for Chapter 7:

1. Rogers, Carl. A Way of Being. Mariner Books, 1980. p. 142

2. Clark, Arthur, J. "Empathy: an integral model in the counseling process. (Practice & Theory)" Journal of Counseling and Development. (June 22, 2010).

3. Kirsch I, Deacon BJ, Huedo-Medina TB, Scoboria A, Moore TJ, et al. 2008 Initial Severity and Antidepressant Benefits: A Meta-Analysis of Data Submitted to the Food and Drug Administration. PLoS Med 5(2): e45. doi:10.1371/journal.pmed.0050045

Chapter 8 ~ Identifying Your Own Energy

Intuition is an internal guidance system that we are all blessed with. All of us are able to tap into our inner strength and call upon our higher power at any given moment. However, some people trust their intuition and pay attention to their instinctual inner guidance more than others. As a society, we have been conditioned to ignore or repress our feelings, and we've been taught that our emotions are not trustworthy. I've found the exact opposite to be true.

Our ancestors used their intuition to survive, whether it was to help them find food, predict weather, or know when to hide or flee. Our intuition can signal a warning to help us steer away from a dangerous person or situation. It can also help us make decisions when an opportunity is presented. Just think how many times you have thought, "If only I had listened to myself, or I should have followed my gut feeling."

Getting information from your intuition can come subtly in the form of ideas, thoughts, emotions, a sense of knowing, an internal voice, a gut feeling, or through the physical senses. Have you ever had a situation where all the facts looked like things were in order, but inwardly you felt that something wasn't quite right or on the up and up? What do you do when your gut feeling goes against the flow or discloses something deeper or hidden? Do you pay attention to it, or do you ignore it? The more you pay attention to it, the more you will learn to recognize your own internal guidance, and the more in touch with your own energy and body you will be.

Having empathic ability does not necessarily mean you are a psychic. It simply means that you have an innate talent, just like an artist who can create a beautiful work of art. You may not be able to play the piano the first time you sit at the keyboard, but you can take lessons and learn. This chapter is to help you build what professors Peter Salovey and John D. Mayer define as "emotional intelligence" or the ability to "monitor one's own and others' feelings and emotions, to discriminate among them, and to use this information to guide one's thinking and actions."[1]

Recognizing that you're an empath is the first step in taking charge of your emotions instead of constantly drowning in them. The most challenging thing about developing and honing empathic abilities is learning to discern what energetic stuff is yours, and what belongs to someone else. Chronic anxiety, depression, or stress wears down our defenses and makes us even more susceptible to the negative energy of others, especially those with similar unresolved emotional issues. In some cases, you may be dealing with a combination of your own stuff and someone else's.

My adult son, Zeb, is an auto mechanic. One hot, humid summer day, he was working under the hood of a car in a shop that had no air-conditioning when he suddenly began having heart palpitations, headache, and nausea. His muscles were tense and cramping, his skin was hot and flushed, he had difficulty breathing, and felt tired, fevered, confused, and dizzy. Knowing something was horribly wrong, he went to the emergency room where he learned he was suffering from heat exhaustion after becoming dehydrated. A week later, he was still not feeling well. He had started having panic attacks and the heart palpitations had returned; so, he decided to see a doctor. His EKG and other tests came back normal, but I could tell he was upset about something. He's not one to offer unsolicited information so I quizzed him and learned that three days prior, his boss had suffered a heart attack at work. Zeb had found him slumped over in the front seat of a customer's car and begun administering CPR while waiting for the paramedics to arrive. During this incident, Zeb's compassionate heart energy wandered into his boss's energy field and picked up on the man's panic and fear. The auto repair shop where he was working was already struggling financially. Having the boss out of the office indefinitely meant a loss of job security for my son. Therefore, he was carrying his boss's fearful energy, as well as his own fear of not having income while the shop was closed. I taught my son how to avoid tapping into the energy field of others, but being an untrained and compassionate empath, he had been picking up "stuff" like this all his life. Like mother, like son. There was so much detrimental energy in his field, I sent him to my friend, Sally Hinkle, who calls her work Transformative Energy Therapy. She was able to remove quite a bit of clutter from Zeb's auric field and open his chakras. As a result, my son's self-esteem blossomed. He is now an entrepreneur who successfully operates his own automotive business in Nashville.

Here are some ways to identify and distinguish your own energy from that of another person.

1. **Ask**. If you are feeling overwhelmed by emotions, the first thing to do is ask yourself if the feeling is yours or someone else's. If you are angry with someone, the feeling is probably your own, but you could also be participating in the energy of the person you quarreled with. Try to resolve the situation, forgive, and let it go. If the energy is not yours, try to determine the obvious originator. Whenever we are in close proximity to another person, our energy fields overlap. For example, if you are feeling out of whack and you've just witnessed an accident or have been in a crowded public setting, you may have picked up the feelings of other people. If possible, move at least twenty feet away from the suspected source and notice whether you feel relief. Center yourself by concentrating on your breath—exhaling negativity and inhaling peace. Draw your aura in closer by visualizing it extending no more than two feet from your body until you get home. Then, ground yourself using the techniques discussed in Chapter 9. This can bring relief very quickly.

2. **Intuition practice exercise.** The word "intuition" is the noun form of the verb "to intuit," which comes from Latin, meaning "to look in" or "to look on." Here is an exercise to help you look in on your intuition and use it as a guidance tool when you are faced with making a decision.

Think about a situation you are currently in. Perhaps you are about to launch into a new business venture, or make a change in residence, or leave/begin a relationship. You probably have at least two choices to make: either go for it or turn away the opportunity—at least for the time being.

Take a deep breath to center your thoughts and become aware of your feelings. As you release the breath, hold the thought that you will accept the opportunity being presented to you.

Now think of the situation again and consider turning away the opportunity. Did you feel an inward shift?

Which thought made you feel peaceful, happy, or relaxed?

Which thought made you feel tense, uneasy, or agitated?

Did you notice yourself wanting to hold your breath when considering either thought?

The thought that made you feel relaxed or at ease is more than likely the choice you should make.

Fear should not be a factor in any decision you make. Feeling fear when you are considering your options could mean that you are picking up on the energy of another person—perhaps someone is urging you to make a decision that you really don't think is best, but you are afraid of the consequences of disappointing them. Being true to yourself means making the decision that is best for you and your divine path.

Once you find that feeling of contentment regarding a decision you are about to make, continue to hold that sensation and get used to how it feels. This is your instructive instinct. This is spiritual guidance or intuition that you can learn to trust and follow.

Pay attention to the feelings and impressions you receive wherever you go. You may have a feeling that you don't want to go into a certain place, or you don't want to connect with a certain person. You are wise to trust those feelings; they come to us for a reason, whether it makes rational sense or not. Intuition does not come from the rational side of our brain; it comes from a place of higher knowing that is meant to guide us and keep us safe.

3. Spend time building a relationship with yourself. The busier we get the less we are likely to take time to sit still and listen to the voice within, but this is a very important part of learning to sense your own energy and honing your intuitive skills. We may be doing something wonderful for someone else, but if we neglect taking time to renew our own energy, we put ourselves at risk of being overwhelmed. Self-healing and self-care is a wonderful gift we can offer ourselves as empathic healers. Taking a break, spending time in meditation, and relaxing are some of the best ways to get to know how your energy feels, raise your vibration, and avoid taking on other's symptoms.

Gini Grey, a transformational coach and the author of *From Chaos to Calm: How to Shift Unhealthy Stress Patterns and Create Your Own Balance in Life*, offers four suggestions to heal emotional pain by getting to know yourself, your sensations, and emotions.[2]

1. Body scan. Spend fifteen minutes each day in a quiet setting where you can close your eyes and turn inward. Begin by focusing on your breath. Feel it come in through your nostrils, expanding your lungs and diaphragm. Then scan your body from head to toes, limb by limb, noticing any sensations. Start with surface skin sensations and then go deeper to feel the tingling of energy flowing through your body. This will support you to be in the present moment and become more comfortable and acceptant of your body sensations.

2. **Meditation breaks**. Throughout the day, do quick, easy meditations where you stop to notice your breathing, thoughts, and emotions that are currently arising. Without judging anything as good or bad, just notice what is occurring for a few minutes and then go back to your work. See if you can bring present moment awareness to your daily tasks.

3. **Bring presence to emotions**. As you become more mindful of what is occurring for you in the present moment, you will begin to sense emotions as they arise. Before they take over and consume you, or you try to cover them up with thinking, eating, or busyness, simply be with them. Observe them with neutrality. What sensations are connected to them? Do you feel tightness, resistance, hollowness, or some other physical experience? Where in your body do they reside? We tend to resist emotions we want to avoid, but suffering is a direct result of resistance to painful emotions that are stuck within us. These feelings have messages to give us if we stop long enough to listen. Once we understand them, we can let go of any stories around them and just be present and accept them as they are. Non-resistance will bring healing. I hate to use such a ridiculous and gross analogy, but have you've ever been sick to your stomach and thought if you could just throw up, you would feel better? It's the same with stuck emotions. Once you get rid of them, you are on your way to healing.

4. **Embrace painful emotions**. When you feel ready to touch into deeper emotional pain, put aside an hour to honor yourself and process emotions. You may want to begin with a meditation technique to relax your body, calm your mind, and connect to your spiritual self. From this centered space, explore your body for

old emotional pain that wants to be heard, acknowledged, and released. It may start as a sensation in your body, or a picture in your mind. Go with it until you touch the emotional aspect. Be gentle, kind, and compassionate with yourself. Remember that you are bigger than any pain or emotion. As painful feelings surface, wrap them in your loving presence. Say hello to them. Feel their depth. If you are visual, you may see the emotion as a shape or color. What message is it trying to convey? Does it want to be released? Let go of any holding or resistance and feel it melt away. What sensation, feeling or emotion is underneath? Stay with this process until you feel complete.

When we radically accept what is without judgment, but with neutrality and compassion, our emotional pain softens, loosens and dissolves. We are then left with our true nature of love and joy.

Another great technique for sensing your own energy is given in Chapter 9 under the heading "Aura or Body Shield."

Sources for Chapter 8:

1. Salovey, Peter and John D. Mayer. Emotional Intelligence, page 189. Dude Publishing, 2004.

2. Grey, Gini. "Healing Emotional Pain with Radical Acceptance." Quips and Tips for Spiritual Seekers. 8 May 2010. Accessed 11 January 2011.
<http://theadventurouswriter.com/quipstipsspiritualseekers/healing-emotional-pain-with-radical-acceptance>.

Chapter 9 ~ Clearing Your Energy Field

Some highly-sensitive people silently show empathy and compassion by soaking up other peoples' negative energy. We naturally want to restore balance and heal people wherever we go, but the trouble is we don't realize that taking negative energy from other folks will eventually make us sick or get us into trouble, as you've read in my personal account. Energy from others first engages with the energetic layers or subtle bodies that create the interconnected electromagnetic field of energy (auric field) around our physical body. Information in this auric field is received by the chakras and sent to the brain for processing and sending messages to the areas of the body that correlate with that type of information. Therefore, clearing your energy field is the place to begin working when you decide you've had enough of taking on everyone else's stuff.

There are many easy and effective ways to control and eliminate detrimental energy and entities that may have entered your field during your workday. If you are employed at a retail store where you encounter customers, or in a hospital or clinic where you tend to those who are sick or dying, you are likely to be affected. Several times, my husband has brought home the ghost of a patient who passed during his shift at the hospital. Let's not even go into the yucky stuff our police force, emergency response teams, victims of violent crimes, and detectives pick up!

Clearing is an ongoing process and must be done regularly to stay free of other people's energy. When you first put defense mechanisms in place, you may still get overwhelmed in a crowd or when there is emotional turmoil around you, but the discomfort will lessen as you continue to develop your intuition. I tried several techniques to help cut down the amount of energy I let into my field. I started with some very basic ones, which worked quite well, so I continued using them. As my knowledge grew, I added new methods. As I continue to discover more helpful techniques, I will post them on my Web site, WeAre1InSpirit.com. You may want to check there from time to time.

The methods in this chapter are things you can do at home, but depending upon how much stuff you have in your field and how long it has been there and how fast you want to get rid of it, you may want to consider receiving some type of energy work from an energy worker or natural health practitioner. There are a wide variety of modalities to choose from: Reiki, sound healing therapy, healing touch, transference healing, hypnotherapy, vibrational therapy, bio-energetic therapy, and many others. See the resources section in the back of this book for a list of providers I trust.

The at-home clearing methods listed here are in alphabetical order to help you easily find the one you are looking for when you use this section as a reference. Some of the methods I share will work better for you than others. If one technique doesn't work, try different ones until something clicks for you. There's no concern about compatibility; these techniques all move in the same direction and ultimately contribute to one result—releasing you from the energetic burdens you have been carrying. Select a method that appeals to you and then notice how you feel. Most of you are so energy sensitive, you will immediately be able to sense a shift. You'll know your field is clearing when you experience a sense of joy and lightness. With a little trial and error, you can learn which methods work best for you and establish a daily practice that helps you maintain your joy. Using these tools has made a world of difference for me. I trust they will help you reach a new level of comfort, control the flow of information you receive, develop emotional intelligence, and avoid being bombarded by unwanted energy.

Private space is very important to energy-sensitive people, so plan to find a place to practice these techniques. Your space should be free of clutter and arranged so it allows energy to flow rather than get stuck. For some really easy tips on how to create a beneficial space using the principles of feng shui, I suggest Tisha Morris' book, *27 Things to Feng Shui Your Home*.

If your space is used by other family members, you may need to cleanse your sacred space before you begin each session. I suggest smudging with sage, lighting incense or a candle, drumming, shaking a percussion rattle, or ringing a bell. Your sacred space will become your personal haven, so make it special. After several sessions, you may notice how positive energy has accumulated in your sacred space and welcomes you each time you enter.

Alone Time

Most empaths are comfortable being alone and even desire to be, but many of us live fast-paced lives that do not include time for contemplation and checking to see what is going on with our emotions, energy, and body. Plan to spend some quiet time alone in your space each day to emotionally release any accumulated negative energy.

If you are away from home, you can take several mini-breaks throughout the day: stretching or taking a short walk outdoors to get some fresh air will help get the energy moving. These interludes will reduce the excessive stimulation going non-stop around you. If you encounter an emotional overload and feel tense or sick, act fast. Pull away to a place (even the restroom if that is the only space you can find to be alone). There, you can ground and center your own energy and remind yourself that you do not take on energy from others.

Affirmations

You can release energy that doesn't belong to you by using affirmations—small but positive messages to the self. They are used as reminders, helping to keep positive messages at the forefront of your consciousness. Not only is it important to regularly repeat these affirmations, it is a great idea to post them in your work environment, where you will notice them. Say the affirmation as if it were already true. What you think about comes about, so be diligent in re-training your thoughts. Affirmations can also create a filter that blocks the detrimental energy of others. Since it is best to make affirmations personal to you, I recommend that you create your own. However, if you're new to this practice, you might enjoy using some of the affirmations I use.

I am willing to feel only the energy that is mine, and I let go of all that is not mine.

I receive energy that is of the highest good for me, and I am protected from all other energy.

I keep my auric field at two and a half feet from my body.

My auric boundary is strong.

I hear, see, feel, and sense only the emotional information that is important for me to know and act upon.

I am honored and respected by all.

I am always safe and divinely protected.

Everything I need to know is revealed to me.

I am vibrantly healthy as I carry positive energy and thoughts.

I am abundantly blessed and happy as I express the beauty and creativity of my heart.

I clearly communicate my needs and take the time necessary to appreciate my own energy, know my true self, and grow spiritually.

I attract only kind and gentle life lessons and relationships into my life.

I understand the divine plan for my life. I have passion and energy to fulfill it with joy!

Aura or Body Shield

Around your physical body, there is a magnetic shield of energy known as your aura. Its purpose is to provide protection and gather energy and information as you interface with your environment. In grade school, we had to be reminded to keep our hands to ourselves! The same is true with the energy field surrounding our body. Ideally, it should be kept two to three feet from the body, but many untrained empaths unknowingly allow their aura to extend and blend with the energy fields of others who have lax boundaries around their auras. We can tap into the thoughts in emotional impulses of someone across the world. An energy worker told me about a client whose auric field extended for about four city blocks! The client was an emotional mess. Anxiety attacks, illnesses, negativity, fear, dread, anger—you name it, she felt it. She worked with the client to clear her field and bring her aura in closer to her body. When her aura was still extended about one block, the client said she felt like she was smothering.

It is important to clear your aura before bringing it in closer to your body or you may entrap all the junk you have picked up while "roaming." Begin by visualizing divine white light surrounding your body and aura. This light is clearing and balancing all aspects of your being. Next establish a grounding cord of any color you choose. Let a shower of golden sunlight flow in your aura for five minutes while you meditate or rest.

Next, close your eyes and try to determine where your energy field (aura) ends. Then, visualize yourself drawing it in closer to your body. Note any sensations or changes you feel. Continue to draw your auric field in, closer and closer. Continue until you sense it is between two and three feet from your body. If you have to stop because you feel uncomfortable, clear your field with the shower of golden sunlight again and repeat the clearing and drawing in process later that day or try again the next day. Continue these sessions until you achieve the ideal range. This exercise can make a huge difference in how much energy you pick up. The less you pick up, the less you have to clear later.

Chakras

Located alongside the spine, there are multiple wheel-like energy centers or vortices that fan outward from key points in your body into the subtle bodies of your auric field. The chakras receive and transmit energy and information from your environment. The chakras can affect the energetic, physical, emotional, spiritual and intellectual aspects of a person. There are seven major chakras, each correlating to a different aspect.

The **root** chakra, located at the base of your spine, is about survival, the ability to earn a living, feeling at home, being present in your body, or accepted in situations.

The **sacral** chakra, located half way between the root chakra and the navel, is about passion, intimacy, and sexuality. When this chakra is open, you are able to easily express and are comfortable with expressing your passion for life. Empaths who have an over-active sacral chakra tend to be extremely emotional.

The **solar plexus** chakra, located just above the navel, is about self-expression and self-esteem. It has to do with how passive or aggressive you are, and your ability to make decisions and interact in groups. Negative emotions such as fear frequently lodge here.

The **heart** chakra, located in the middle of the chest, is about love and relationships.

The **throat** chakra, located in the neck area, is about self-expression and communication.

The **third-eye** chakra, located in the middle of the forehead near the eyebrows, has to do with insight, thought, and visualization.

The **crown** chakra, located in the crown of the head, is the seat of spirituality and connects us to divine wisdom and intellect.

I recommend Harriette Knight's book, *CHAKRA POWER! How to Fire Up Your Energy Centers to Live a Fuller Life,* for more information about how the chakras operate.

The aura and chakras can become blocked, unbalanced, and damaged through negative energy, repressed emotions, entities, toxins, drug and alcohol abuse, and traumatic experiences. You can test to see how open or active your chakras are by answering a few questions at http://www.eclecticenergies.com/chakras/chakratest.php. If your chakras need a lift, place your palm on the weak chakra and send pink light to that area. For longstanding depression or anxiety, use this method daily to strengthen any chakra.

Nature always tries to achieve perfect balance. Clearing your aura and chakras will help this natural effort considerably, but if there is extensive damage to the aura or chakras, you may need assistance from a qualified energy worker who can cleanse, balance, heal, and restore them. A list of recommended providers can be found in the resources section near the end of this book. If energy work is out of the question for you, try listening to chakra clearing music (see resources).

Bathe in Salt Water

Fill a bathtub with warm water and add one handful of all-natural sea salt (available at health food stores, department stores, etc.). Soak in the bath, making sure that you submerge fully at least once. This not only helps relax the body and draw out toxins, it will remove contaminants from your aura and other energetic fields. If you are not at a place where you can take a tub bath, take a shower and envision all negative energy being cleansed from you.

Breathe

Breathing is necessary to sustain life. When we are tense or stressed we tend to hold our breath, but this only makes things worse. Conscious and focused breathing can release pent up negative energy. Five minutes of deep breaths while counting your inhalations and your exhalations can help restore a sense of calmness and regulate the heartbeat. Controlling and counting the breaths develops the concentration and focus needed to manage mental noise. Do this while sitting in a comfortable position with your spine straight.

The Book of Storms by Jadoa Alexander teaches empathic breathing, in which the breath begins by inhaling slowly through your nostrils, filling your lungs from the bottom up. When your lungs are full without straining, hold your breath to the count of four. Exhale slowly by blowing out a long silent whistle. Empty your lungs as much as you can without straining, then hold to the count of four. This cycle is considered one breath. Repeat up to ten times, relaxing and breathing normally between breaths if you need to. The goal is to build up to three sets of ten breaths, but whatever number you are able to do without feeling uncomfortable will start to work for you.

Whenever I do a breathing exercise, I sense myself moving through different states of consciousness, which really helps to quiet my mind and turn down the mental chatter in my head. If things are coming up for healing and I really sense a need for deeper clearing of old or stuck energy, I will use the breathing technique that invokes the Divine Mother energy. This is known as Liberation Breathing® as taught by Sondra Ray. See the rebirthing exercise in this chapter or visit sondraray.com.

By taking in more life force through the breath, limiting thoughts and memories that cause problems and disease are released. This conscious, connected breathing process produces extraordinary healing results.

Centering

Being spiritually centered means living aligned with Spirit/Source instead of fear-based ego. By viewing life through spiritual eyes, you can see the bigger picture and feel peaceful while seeing all the possibilities that exist in a situation. When I am centered, I feel present in my body, expansive, one with Source and everything that exists. I am able to be present in my body and allow my emotions to surface so I may process them (non-resistant). I am able to tune out unwanted external noise and tune in to the gentle inner voice of intuition that helps me make better decisions.

I have included the centering exercise in the grounding exercise because they go hand in hand. One needs to be done with the other for maximum effect.

Crystals and Gemstones

I have a bowl of gemstones that I love toying with. I lay them out in a circle or row and intuitively decide which one has the energy I need to clear or protect myself at that time. My daughter-in-law, Amanda, is a jewelry artisan with a shop on Etsy.com (http://www.etsy.com/shop/eidolajewelry). I've had her custom-design several of my favorite crystals into pendants that I can interchange on a silver neck chain. I almost always wear a necklace or carry a gemstone in my pocket when I go out into public. I even wear them at home because I love the positive energy they emit.

Essential Oils

The oils that plants contain are essential to their growth and have distinct properties that can be used to enhance the health and well-being of your body, emotions, aura, or physical space. About twelve years ago, I learned about the benefits of using essential oils for healing and clearing. I mixed all kinds of recipes and made soap, bath salts, bath oils, candles, room fresheners, and personal fragrances. Some of my favorites are neroli, bergamot, sandalwood, rosewood, patchouli, myrrh, and of course lavender and rose! Each essential oil has different properties. Sage, peppermint, cedar, thyme, eucalyptus, and rosemary are all great for clearing. Chamomile, orange, and lavender are wonderfully calming. A drop or two placed on your pillow at night may help you enjoy a more restful sleep. Not all essential oils can be applied directly to the skin, so I highly suggest that you study the art of aromatherapy rather than using these oils haphazardly. See the resources section for a list of books on using essential oils.

Flower Essence Remedies

Flower essence remedies can be used for easing emotional upsets and calming sensitivities associated with being an empath. Olive, yarrow, beech, mountain pennyroyal, dandelion, borage, heather, fawn lily, mallow, yellow star tulip, and manzanita are most commonly used for releasing emotionally-charged energies, creating gentle energy shifts, balancing emotions, and shielding yourself from foreign energies. See the resources section for information about flower essences.

Forgiveness

This may seem like an odd place to mention forgiveness, but in order to know how forgiveness can clear your emotions, bring healing, and raise your vibration, you need to understand what unforgiveness or any other repressed emotion does to your energy field. Have you ever noticed how awful you feel after you've had an argument with someone? Regardless of who lost or won (everyone loses when anger is used to manipulate an outcome), you may continue to relive the incident and obsess over the situation instead of simply forgiving the offense and moving on. Energy attracts energy similar to itself. It does not matter what the form your anger takes—sarcasm, criticism, judgment, apathy, depression—carrying around an energetic burden of anger, fear, sadness, or vengeance lowers your vibration and attracts like energy. When you are angry with another person, you continue to send negative energy to them, and guess what? Whatever you send out, comes back to you, magnified. Even after you stuff an emotion deeply enough that you no longer feel it, it is still alive and actively destroying your aura and chakras as well as causing damage to your physical body.

When someone acts wrongly, he is actually giving you an opportunity to bless him *and* yourself. You need the same forgiveness you offer him. In fact, there is no way to accept forgiveness without offering it because whatever you deny others is exactly what you lack. When you deny forgiveness you will feel deprived. The only way to get rid of this kind of detrimental energy is to offer forgiveness to everyone. Here's how according to lesson 122 in *A Course in Miracles*:

> *Begin by thinking of someone you do not like, who seems to irritate you; one you actively despise, or merely try to overlook.*
>
> *Now close your eyes and see him in your mind, and look at him a while. Try to perceive some light in him somewhere; a little gleam that you have never noticed. Try to find some little spark of brightness shining through the ugly picture that you hold of him. Look at this picture until you see a light somewhere within it, for in that light his holiness shows you your savior, saved and saving, healed and whole. Now try to expand this light until it covers him and makes the picture beautiful and good. Then let him offer you the light you see in him.*
>
> *Look at this changed perception for a while, and then turn your mind to someone you consider a friend. Try to transfer the light you learned to see around your former "enemy" to this friend. Let your "enemy" and friend unite in blessing you with what you have given them. Now are you one with them, and they with you. Now you have been forgiven by*

yourself.

*Do not forget, throughout the day, the role
forgiveness plays in bringing happiness to
your mind.*

I realize there are some abusive situations that are
difficult to forgive—in fact, it is impossible for the ego
to forgive anything or let go of an offense. Only by
allowing Spirit to address the situation can forgiveness
come forth. True forgiveness is not overlooking the
"bad" in a person; it is about letting go of anything that
keeps you from experiencing peace of mind. This
means giving up "attack" thoughts and not taking
things personally or projecting your expectations on to
others. It means not seeing yourself as a victim, who
has been attacked, abandoned, betrayed,
misunderstood, etc. You have to release the personal
thought system (ego) by recognizing your oneness with
Spirit/Source and others. This is not something we can
grasp intellectually. We must allow Spirit/Source into
our awareness over and over until love becomes a real
experience. When you are centered in Spirit, you can
simply observe abusive behavior and recognize that this
person is behaving that way because of something
going on in his or her mind; it has nothing to do with
you. You can then decide to be around this
person/behavior or not. Remaining in an
uncomfortable or dangerous situation is self-torture,
not forgiveness. Your choice to no longer speak with
this person is a miracle, not a failure! A miracle shifts
your mind toward peace, away from conflict.
Forgiveness and peace show up as a result of your
choice to take care of yourself by avoiding an abusive
person. You can't expect the abusive person to change

his ways. A miracle always occurs in your mind; therefore, a change of mind is all that is needed to bring you peace.

"To release the charge of an emotion is not the same as deleting the memory of the event," writes Luis Angel Diaz on page 14 in his book, *Memory in the Cells.* "It involves liberating the trapped vital force in order to use it for growth and self-healing."[1]

Grounding

Gini Grey says it best, "Much like an electrical appliance needs to be grounded in order to operate properly, our body needs to have an energy connection to the earth in order to function optimally. Besides, it feels great to be grounded in the body! Since we naturally ground through the bottoms of our feet, it's no wonder we feel more present, relaxed, and stable when we walk in nature or work in a garden. (There's something therapeutic about working in the dirt or playing in the sand!) This energetic grounding cord is invisible to the naked eye, but it flows from the root chakra at the base of the spine and flows all the way down to the center of the earth. Simply bringing your awareness to it and intending to have it flow is all you need to do to ground your energy."

Staying grounded in your own energy and bringing in higher vibrational energy is critical to empaths. Here are some very effective grounding and centering techniques that I use every day:

Imagine a wide cylinder of white light extending from the higher realms above you, encasing your body and aura. The light is going through you, and passing into the very center of the earth where it locks in place. You are surrounded by this light and nothing negative can penetrate it. Because this light is above you, in you, around you, and below you, it is grounding you to the earth's energy, clearing your aura, and raising your vibration by connecting with higher realms.

Imagine that you are growing roots from the bottom of your feet that reach deep in the earth. These roots are flexible, so when you lift your feet, the roots follow you.

See a cord of light (you choose the color) coming from your root chakra and extending deep into the earth.

Go outside and actually touch the ground with your hands or feet. Sit on the ground if weather and soil conditions permit. Visualize all the negative energy you have accumulated during the day moving out of your body through your hands, feet, or buttocks and going into the earth where it is absorbed and neutralized.

To experience the difference between being grounded and ungrounded, try this exercise that Gini Grey shares on her Web site, http://www.ginigrey.com:

Stand to your feet and consciously imagine having an energy cord going from your root chakra all the way down to the center of the earth. Allow it to be as wide as your hips. Notice how it feels in your body as you stand as still as possible. Now, lift one foot. You are probably pretty well balanced while grounded. Now, try purposely ungrounding your energy by pulling the grounding cord up or disintegrating it so you are no longer grounded. Now try standing on one foot and notice how you feel. Ground yourself again and notice the difference. When you are grounded, you feel deeply connected to yourself and at peace with everything around you.[2]

Herbal Therapy

Teas and herbs have interested me for a long time. I feel that I may have worked with herbs in another lifetime, which has been further extended in this lifetime through my love of gardening. I grow lemon balm, basil, white sage, echinacea, mint, verbena, bee balm, and black-eyed Susan. There are a wide variety of uses for herbs in a spiritual and healing practice from cleansing the body, restoring health, and clearing a space. I won't go into detail about them in this book; however, I encourage you to seek more information if herbology interests you. See the books listed in the resources section of this book.

Light

Whenever I feel uneasy or am about to go into a public setting where I may encounter a high influx of energy from others, I visualize Divine white light extending from the highest realms of the universe to the center of Gaia—Mother Earth. This light surrounds my body and aura, as it clears and balances all aspects of my being. I establish a grounding cord of the color I feel impressed is right for the situation. I draw in my aura size to about two feet from my body.

I ask for a shower of golden sunlight to flow through my aura for about two minutes while I visualize the Christ-gold light and Archangel Michael's blue light surrounding me. I ask Archangel Chamuel to help lost souls find their way to the light without my having to be consciously involved in the process. Finally, before leaving home, I ask for the violet flame of St. Germaine to surround the outer boundary of my aura to transmute any negative energy into an energy form that is beneficial for me, my body, my life, and others.

Meditation

Meditation is very helpful for getting centered and getting to know what is going on within you. Many times we get so busy that we forget to check in and sense our own energy. Meditation is the practice of taking the time to be still and listen to the voice within. In meditation we receive guidance, inspiration, ideas, and what I call "downloads" of information that we can use to consciously co-create our life and world. I like to use a candle when I meditate because gazing into the flame quiets my mind and allows me to shut out the distractions around me. I also enjoy burning incense, which helps clear my personal space. It has become so associated with my meditation practice that whenever I smell Nag Champa, I automatically want to stop what I'm doing and be still.

Meditation allows us to receive energy from higher realms and to run our own energy through our chakras. It would be nice to be able to meditate for hours a day, but unless you are a monk or nun you probably have a family to feed, kids to carpool, errands to run, and a career to tend to. If you are willing to take eleven minutes a day to meditate and work on your spiritual self, I highly recommend *Twenty Gems, Journey to the Self* by Denna Shelton. These DVDs and digital downloads can be played at work, on a laptop computer, and on your iPhone or iPad. The beautiful nature scenery, mesmerizing animations, soothing music, and positive affirmations combine to give a refreshing lift to your spirit.

Music and Sound

Take your focus away from earth-bound thought patterns by surrounding yourself with music. Sound is the vibration of life. Flow with it. Give yourself permission to sing along, relax, take a nap, dance, or whatever you feel led to do. Shaking a rattle, beating a drum, playing an instrument, chiming a Tibetan bowl, or making a gentle or repetitive sound can also help you clear your chakras, aura, and body. See the resources section for recommendations.

Nature

When my husband and I were taking courses through American Institute of Holistic Theology in 2003, we each chose an elective as part of the curriculum. He chose a course in feng shui and I chose mandala art. This proved to be a perfect combination for us. We used the knowledge gained from these studies to create a mandala garden based upon the Chinese feng shui elements of color, direction, and symbols.

Since then, we have built an altar to the Divine Mother in the center of the garden. There, we perform rituals and offer gifts of fruits, flowers, herbs, vegetables, incense, fire, water, stones, shells, and other items to show our love and appreciation for the beauty of nature and the Divine Mother's protection and ability to sustain our physical lives. The energy in the garden is so strong that I am immediately made aware of the sacredness of the space and do not enter it without being mindful. This special place has no negative energy. Just being in the space seems to clear my entire aura and refresh my body.

I encourage you to create a space in your yard or garden, on your patio, balcony, or deck where you can be alone in nature and connect with the loving energy of Mother Goddess. If nothing else, stand barefoot in the grass for a few moments.

Prayer

Prayer is an important part of any spiritual practice because it offers the opportunity to petition the divine source, which is always positive, uplifting, and beneficent. Though it is hard to believe sometimes, entities do respect free will and respond to prayers that ask them to leave. Regardless of whether you believe in entities or not, these methods do work to remove detrimental influences of all kinds. These practices cannot do you any harm or cause retaliation. If you sense you are being affected by an entity or dark energy—recite a prayer as often as necessary. Here are a few examples:

> *As I leave home today, I will not sense other people's feelings or pain. I ask my angels or spirit guides to put white light around me to prevent me from picking up energy that is not beneficial to me. The Light will heal and bless others as it protects me.*

> *Father/Mother/God/Spirit/Source, I ask that all souls, energy patterns, and entities be sent on their spiritual evolution for the highest good and mutual benefit of everyone concerned.*

"The Great Invocation" written by Alice Bailey[3] is a world prayer, translated into almost seventy languages and dialects. It is an instrument of power to aid the plan of God in finding full expression on Earth. To use it is an act of service to humanity and the Christ. It expresses certain central truths, which all people innately and normally accept. See http://www.lucistrust.org/invocation for details.

*From the point of Light within the Mind of
God, let Light stream forth into the minds of
men. Let Light descend on Earth.*

*From the point of Love within the Heart of
God, let love stream forth into the hearts of
men. May Christ return to Earth.*

*From the center where the Will of God is
known, let purpose guide all little wills of
men—the purpose which the Masters know
and serve.*

*From the center which we call the race of men,
let the plan of Love and Light work out. And
may it seal the door where evil dwells.*

*Let Light and Love and Power restore the Plan
on Earth.*

Raise Your Vibration

Slower vibrating energies cannot reach you when you
vibrate at a faster level than they do. It's like you
become invisible to these energy leeches. Here's how:

See the light within yourself near your heart center.
Visualize that circle of light growing brighter and
brighter as it expands to encircle your body. It extends
from your body and fills the room you are in. Next, it
expands as large as your house. Continue to see this
light growing larger to fill your entire neighborhood,
city, county, state, continent, and finally the whole
Earth and universe. Now see your light joining with the
cosmic light of the angels, archangels, Christ and the
ascended masters (avatars or perfected beings), and
God/Goddess. Allow their light to fill the circle of light
surrounding you and raise your vibration. Now, begin
to pull this light into your being as the circle of light

shrinks to the size of the Earth, your continent, state, county, city, neighborhood, and your room. Bring your light-filled aura closer until it extends only about two and a half feet from your body.

Read

I love to read books that inspire, uplift, and encourage me to expand my mind and grow spiritually. Some books, such as *The Four Agreements* by Don Miguel Ruiz, have altered my life's philosophy and how I approach relationships. *The Pleiadian Workbook* by Amora Quan Yin gave me some great ideas about how to ground and center myself and introduced me to working with ascended masters and a spiritual guidance team that includes angels, Pleiadian emissaries of light, Jesus, Archangels Michael, Chamuel, and the Violet Flame of St. Germaine. Gregg Braden's book, *The Spontaneous Healing of Belief, Shattering the Paradigm of False Limits*, I learned just how important my feelings, emotions, and beliefs are in manifesting the life I live.

I got a copy of *A Course in Miracles* (*ACIM*) many years ago. I tried to read it then, but for some reason it just didn't resonate with me and I couldn't make practical application of the text. However, after the flood in Nashville in May 2010, I began a serious reading of *A Course in Miracles* and even my husband has noticed a difference in how I process life and its many issues.

Rebirthing

As an author, spiritual teacher, international speaker, and healer with an expertise in the area of relationships, Sondra Ray has been in the forefront of spiritual healing for thirty-five years. Often referred to as the "Mother of Rebirthing," Sondra launched into international acclaim in the 1970s as one of the pioneers of the rebirthing experience. Never before had any training explained how our conception, gestation, and birth trauma affects one's body, relationships, career, and life.

I had a rebirthing session with Sondra Ray and her husband, Mark Sullivan, before having them as guests on my podcast. Using a simple, upper chest circular breathing pattern, you can be liberated from thoughts that cause tension, pain, unpleasant symptoms, and disease. Through rebirthing, you can also let go of addictions, depression, negative patterns in relationships, and even trauma from birth. The benefits of rebirthing are very profound. When we breathe this way, approximately 70 percent of our toxins are released through breathing, rather than through the other eliminative organs.

Be prepared for the ego's attempt to stop you or cause you to alter your breathing so that the rebirthing does not work. It is not uncommon for locking of the jaws to occur in an effort to block the emotions that are surfacing. During my session, I felt myself breathing out mental and emotional blocks, fear, and traumatic incidents from my past. Also, be prepared for some strong repressed emotions to surface. These could overwhelm you. It took weeks for me to integrate the energy shift that resulted in my first session. It also led me to a renewal in my daily spiritual practice and peace of mind. Plan to commit to enough sequential sessions (ten is suggested) to dissolve your emotional repression enough to break through. Having a breath coach is useful, not because the method cannot be learned alone or done alone, but because there is some resistance that may be best worked through with the support of someone who is skilled or who has gone through rebirthing. For more information, read Sondra's book, *Celebration of Breath: Rebirthing, Book II; Or How to Survive Anything and Heal Your Body* or Leonard Orr's book, *Rebirthing in the New Age.*

Staying Present

Our mind is easily obsessed with thoughts of the past or future. We tend to "zone out" while driving, or think about our to-do list while walking the dog. I caught myself about to put the milk in the cabinet and the cereal in the refrigerator one morning! We don't really listen when we are talking to someone. We have to continually bring our awareness back to the current moment as we go through the day in order to create a habit of being aware of what is happening to us energetically. Mindfulness, whether you are eating, driving, or cleaning the house, involves being present with the task at hand instead of being lost in thought. (So much for multi-tasking!) Examples include feeling the warm water running through your fingers as you wash your hands; noticing the difference between true hunger sensations or the urge to sooth painful emotions with comfort food; sensing anger surfacing within before unconsciously lashing out at someone.

When we are aware of what is happening in the present moment our emotions will naturally surface to be released. Most of us do not accept sadness, fear, and anger as a normal part of our human experience. We tend to repress these emotions by being busy, watching TV, playing video games, eating, drinking alcohol, or doing drugs. We also tend to suppress amusement, joy and enthusiasm as if there is something wrong with being "too" happy. When we are able to stay present, we are aware of subtle energy shifts around us or know when we are picking up unwanted energy. This means you can clear it before it becomes a problem.

Smudging

I've been using a Native American tradition called smudging for many years. The technique is very simple and can be used to clear a person, animal, or space. You will need a match or lighter, a small bundle of herbs or a handful of loose leaves such as sage, rosemary, thyme, or cedar; and a bowl or saucer to catch any ashes. Herb bundles are available at herb stores, metaphysical shops, and online markets. I purchased some excellent white sage on Amazon.com.

Place the herbs in a bowl and light the leaves or bundle. Allow the flame to extinguish on its own, or blow it out after about fifteen seconds. Be aware that a glass or metal container will get hot even though the herbs are smoldering and not afire. A pottery mug with a handle works quite well for this purpose. Then use your hand or a feather wand to fan the smoke around the subject you want to clear. Begin with the top of the head and move to the feet, directing the smoke to cover the entire body of the person or animal. If you are clearing a room, direct the smoke into all corners, toward the ceiling, and the floor as you walk around your house or apartment in a counter-clockwise fashion. You may feel a sudden shift as an entity is expelled into the smoke. You can say a prayer to further your intent to remove any stagnant or unhealthy energy.

Violet Flame of St. Germain

The violet flame (also called the violet fire) is a unique

spiritual energy that can help you in all areas of your life. It can heal emotional and physical problems, improve your relationships, help you to grow spiritually, or just make life easier. I have found the Violet flame of St. Germain (Lord of the Seventh Ray) very useful for transmuting detrimental energy into beneficial energy. Simply call upon the ascended master, St. Germain, when you feel that you are being adversely influenced by the impulses, thoughts, or energy from the collective consciousness and ask him to bring his violet flame to you. Or, you can send detrimental energy to his flame. Like the refiner's fire, it will remove the dross and bring forth pure gold. It transmutes energy around me without my having to be actively or consciously aware that I am helping or healing others, and because it also acts as a shield, it keeps me from picking up unwanted psychic information or energy.

Visualization and Guided Meditation

There are too many excellent CDs to list them all, but meditations that guide you inward to a place where healing abides is a great way to unwind and find your place of peaceful stillness. The background music makes the experience even more peaceful, but you don't have to use a commercially made music CD. I've made some recordings of my own voice leading me into a place of deep peace and quiet. You can do a grounding visualization at any time. Imagine that you are growing roots from the bottom of your feet. The roots are reaching deeper into the earth, but they're flexible. You can lift your feet and the root will follow you as you walk about. You just grounded your energy using your inner sight. Wasn't that easy?

Writing/Journaling

Janet Conner's book *Writing Down Your Soul: How to Activate and Listen to the Extraordinary Voice Within* has made an impact upon my journaling because it takes me beyond writing down my daily problems to really connecting with my soul and discovering what Spirit is saying to me on a soul level. I attended a lecture at First Church Unity in Nashville where Janet shared how to use the following seven steps to get into theta brain wave:

1. Set your intention to connect with the voice inside you.

2. Address the voice directly: Dear _____ (fill in the blank with whatever name you want).

3. Write by hand.

4. Activate all five senses. Vision, hearing, and touch are automatic in this process, but include a candle, incense, aroma oil, or flowers for smell and water for taste.

5. Ask open-ended questions as you write.

6. Write fast; don't stop to correct grammar, spelling, or punctuation (very hard for me as an editor). Just let the words flow from spirit to paper without the interference of logic or correctness.

7. Be grateful; say thank you.[4]

By reading her book and applying the lessons in a practice of writing, I learned how to get out of my conscious, stress-filled mind, get in touch with my deep, authentic self, and activate a limitless supply of intelligence, wisdom, and creativity.

Yoga

One of the best spiritual practices is yoga because it incorporates grounding, centering, breathing, and exercise while raising vibration through connecting with the Divine. Even five minutes a day can help. There are a multitude of good books and instructional DVDs on practicing yoga. See the resources section for a list of yoga books and CDs.

Sources for Chapter 9:

1. Diaz, Luis Angel. Memory in the Cells. iUniverse. 2010.

2. Grey, Gini. "Staying Grounded." Insights & Inspiration. 14 May, 2009. Accessed 6 January 2011. <http://www.ginigrey.com/wp/spiritual-insights/staying-grounded>.

3.Bailey, Alice. "The Great Invocation."

4. Connor, Janet. Personal notes from Janet's lecture at First Church Unity in Nashville, TN. 2008 November.

Chapter 10 ~Setting Boundaries

If someone was trying to break into your house, you would probably call the police, run for your life, grab a weapon, scream, or something! You wouldn't just stand there and allow the intruder to barge in. Yet, we allow the energy of others to invade our personal space, whether it be in our mind, emotions, or physical body. By not stopping this intrusion, you give away your personal energy. We all have the ability to create our own energy without stealing someone else's energy or becoming entangled in a situation that is none of our business. This requires diligent development of our spiritual practice to raise our vibration, and setting boundaries with those who would siphon our energy.

In the previous chapter, we talked about clearing your aura and learned to visualize a radiant, light-filled field of energy around your physical body. Now we will discover how to protect it from invasion. This egg-shaped shield should be about two to three feet from your body. It needs to be flexible and thin enough to let in what serves you, yet thick enough to keep out what doesn't. When the layers of your body shield are thin or have holes in them, you are more easily influenced by environmental stimuli and negativity. Anyone who has a healthy self-esteem and maintains strong boundaries with others will most likely have a thicker, stronger aura than someone who is fearful, anxious, shy, stressed, jealous, hateful, or holding on to any other negative thought or feeling.

Auras are created from heat and vibration. Similar to how your body raises its temperature while fighting infection, a physical illness can cause a temporary color change or increase in aura size. Containing various colors, each conveying a different meaning, the aura is like a mood ring that changes colors with your physical, psychological, emotional, and spiritual state, as well as by the energies of those around you. If you are unhealthy, there may be shadows, grey, or black areas in your aura or it may appear murky rather than clear and transparent.

Setting Boundaries Around Your Auric Field

Because thoughts are energy, your intention plays a powerful role in all your efforts. The best way to strengthen your personal energy field is to use your thoughts to visualize your aura having a rubber-like quality that causes negativity to bounce off without penetrating. You can consciously change or inject different colors into your aura as needed. Here is a mini guide on using color to strengthen your aura.

Purple: indicates spiritual thoughts.

Blue: balancing, relaxing the nervous system, peace of mind. Can also assist with teaching or presenting information due to its connection with the fifth chakra (communication).

Turquoise: highly energizing, capable of influencing other people, great for multitasking and bringing organization to chaos or scattered thoughts.

Green: restful, peaceful, calming energy, healing. Seen in the aura of those who love gardening.

Yellow: joy, freedom, non-attachment, contentment, releasing, generosity. A yellow halo around the head indicates high spiritual development.

Orange: uplifting, absorbing, inspiring. A sign of power or the ability and/or desire to control someone or a situation.

Red: a predominantly red aura indicates a materialistically-oriented person or one who is concerned about appearances or the physical body.

Pink: spiritual love, a perfect balance between spiritual awareness and material existence. A great color to add to your aura at any time.

White: this color means purity to me but some cultures say it represents death. Your thought and intent is more powerful than what others say or believe.

Experiment with colors and see how they make you feel. The color of clothes you wear can affect your aura. Bright colors enhance your energy and send a silent message. Dull-colored clothes absorb energy and may make you tired quicker.

If you are extremely sensitive, you may need all the colors of a rainbow surrounding you. Visualize a layer of red around your body, then a layer of orange surrounding you, then yellow, green, blue, indigo, violet, and finally a thick layer of white light surrounding all the layers.

Setting Boundaries Using Physical Stance

If you feel that someone or something is trying to drain your energy, you might try taking a physical position to block out external influences. This might include crossing your arms in front of your chest or crossing your legs. Make all your fingers on your left hand touch the fingers on your right hand (think praying hands without the palms touching). Close your eyes, clear your mind, and take long, slow, even breaths until you begin to feel comfortable. It's a way to take a break to refresh and strengthen your body, mind, and aura. Closing off your energy in this way will protect you from negative influences, and keep your energy from reaching other people.

Setting Boundaries with People

Empaths are kind and caring. At times, we are almost saintly because we tend to care for others more than we care for ourselves. However, you are not doing yourself or anyone else any favors by being a martyr. Co-dependency is common in our relationships because we want to please others. Doing or saying something that will make someone else angry or sad is uncomfortable for us, so we often avoid confrontation. After all, if we make someone angry or upset, we will probably pick up that feeling and make us even more uncomfortable. This is not self-care; this is self-sabotage!

Caretaking does not serve or protect another person; it keeps them from growing up and accepting responsibility for their own actions and feelings. You have to be the bad guy from time to time just to maintain your own health and sanity. People may get mad at you if you don't do what they want you to do, but their feelings are not your feelings, and your well-being is not dependent on theirs. Part of maturing as an empath is to stop taking on responsibilities that aren't yours. Judith Orloff MD, (an assistant clinical professor of psychiatry at UCLA) says, "If someone asks too much of you, politely tell them no. It's not necessary to explain why. As the saying goes, 'No is a complete sentence.'"

A person can get so used to caretaking that they feel they are supposed to do it. I believe it is a violation to another person's rights of privacy to even try to pick up or sense things about them unless you first ask their permission. It's like reading their mail or rummaging through their closet! If you are an empath with the typical codependency pattern, your idea of where the line is between you and another person might be a bit blurred. Once you get to know where the line is, it will make all your relationships clearer and cleaner.

Many empaths grew up with parents who were emotionally volatile. One or both parents could erupt without a moment's notice and spew their toxic emotional energy all over us before we could run and hid. We learned to be on guard and get out of the way by sensing the subtle shift in energy when they were about to be upset. As a result, we learned what to say and not say, what to do and not do to make others more at ease so they were safer to be around emotionally and physically. We shifted our tone of voice, spoke softly or not at all, changed our posture or body language so much that we often lost track of what was authentic and true for ourselves. This created an incongruent and confusing internal message.

Because codependency runs in families, we may not have had good role models for setting boundaries. Our diaries, personal space, and belongings were always at risk of being invaded. We learned to live defensively by hiding our stuff, locking our diaries, or avoiding our parents and other people whose energy was uncomfortable. We expanded our intuitive ability to include everyone around us and came to the conclusion that it is normal to meddle in everyone else's emotional stuff. There were probably things that went on behind closed doors in our childhood home that we were not allowed to speak about in public. In order to avoid upsetting people, we learned to keep our mouths shut and may have spent a lot of time alone as children in order to avoid the negativity of family life.

We may know what we need to say or do to set good boundaries, but have a hard time expressing our expectations and following through when these boundaries are being tampered with. The throat chakra is the center for the expression of personal truth. There were times when my throat chakra was so closed, I felt like I could not swallow. My first marriage was all about pretention. We were taught by the churches we attended that we were to project an image of perfect Christian role models for others to follow. Therefore, we never argued or said what we really felt. We tiptoed around issues that needed to be addressed. We didn't seek counseling because that would be like admitting we actually had a problem. During my divorce proceedings and for several months after, I let out years of anger and repressed feelings. Something would trigger a memory that was hurtful and I would start bawling uncontrollably, screaming unmercifully into a pillow, or lashing out at my "imaginary" ex-husband. I've since learned in Luis Angel Diaz' book, *Memory in the Cells*, that this type of activity is a great way to release stuck energy. By admitting what we feel and allowing ourselves to express it in a safe manner (so no one gets hurt) we not only let go of negative energy, we open our throat chakra. By opening the throat chakra, we allow ourselves to expressing our true needs and feelings and let energy move through us rather than getting stuck where it can cause harm.

After my divorce, I gradually learned to stand up for myself without being so emotional. At first, I was all over the place in my attempts to set boundaries. I vacillated between angrily gushing forth whatever I felt at the moment and holding back to avoid hurting other people's feelings. After a while, I learned to speak the truth with loving intention.

Some other good exercises for opening the throat chakra are singing and chanting, sharing your feelings and thoughts with friends (something I was not allowed to do in my first marriage), and meditating on the throat chakra. Some healing stones that help with the throat chakra are turquoise, lapis lazuli, and blue lace agate. You can meditate with them, put them in your pocket, or wear jewelry (particularly necklaces) made of these stones.

Before you leave your home, take a moment to check in with yourself to get a sense of what you feel inside you before you encounter any people in your day. This is your "baseline." If this feeling shifts when you get into public and your find yourself feeling suddenly angry, depressed, sad, or agitated, or even having a sudden headache, tension or other aches and pains, then you may be absorbing energy and emotions from others. Ask yourself if what you are feeling is yours or not. You are in complete control of what you let in and how you let it affect you. If you don't want someone in your energetic field, then you send them away. You set your boundaries and an energetic frequency that is peaceful, calm, and happy. The universal law of attraction insures that as you maintain a vibratory state, others must either match it or go away.

Gini Grey shares four tips for creating healthy boundaries:[1]

1. **Stay centered and grounded**. Being centered and grounded helps release stress. As you interact with others, stay connected to your own inner experience; feel your energy flow through your body, let any foreign energy release down your grounding, and stay centered in your own light vibration. Fill up with your own energy vibration until there's no space for others' problems and pain, but still room for compassion.

2. **Be aware of energy boundaries**. Our energy doesn't end where our skin ends. We each have an electromagnetic field around us called the aura. As you own your aura, you create healthy boundaries around your personal space allowing your own energy to flow freely and prevent others' energy from entering.

3. **Tune into the difference between your emotions and other peoples'**. Empaths take on other peoples' emotions as if they were their own. A friend tells you her husband just filed for divorce and your heart aches. Your brother calls you in a panic about money problems and your stomach twists and turns. You attend a funeral and feel overwhelmed with grief. Like musical notes, each emotion has its own vibration unique to each person. Sadness is lighter than apathy; anger vibrates faster than sadness; amusement feels free and healing; joy is light and bright, and enthusiasm takes you even higher up the scale. Get to know your emotions by feeling them and allowing them to flow. With this awareness you will instantly know when you've taken on someone else's sadness, anger or joy; it won't feel like yours and it won't feel comfortable. Then all you have to do is let it go, like taking off a scarf that isn't yours.

4. **Say goodbye to codependent behaviors**. With big hearts, caretaking and rescuing becomes the norm for empaths. Instead of sensing and feeling another's plight, use your clear seeing abilities to look at your loved one's situation. See who they are beyond their problems and pain; see the spiritual being within who is connected to the Source of all life. Know that just as you have your path to walk, they have theirs. Don't let their victim mask pull you in to taking on their problems. Toss away pity and sympathy, and give the gift of love by shining a light on others' bigness. Allow your friends and family to grow, heal, and evolve through their own struggles and triumphs. If you feel tempted to jump in, reflect back on your life to see if you are projecting any of your own unhealed wounds.

Setting Boundaries with Entities

Some people believe entities are conjured by human thoughts and fed by negative emotional energy. Regardless, of whether others think they are real or imagined, if they bother *you*, then they exist for you and must be dealt with. I don't want to dwell on ghosts in this book, but I know a lot of us deal with the energy of earthbound spirits regardless of whether we see, hear, feel, or sense their presence. Some are spiteful entities who refuse to give up their attachment to the earthly realm.

In *When Ghosts Speak,* Mary Ann Winkowski states that a portal of light is opened whenever someone dies and this window of opportunity remains open for a short while during which a soul can make a choice to go into the light or stay in the earth plane. Some people cross over almost immediately, probably because they were spirituality evolved and had all their loose ends tied up. Others take too much time deciding. They miss their chance to go into the light, and thus become earth bound. As a side note: if ghosts are finding you, and you are willing to help them cross over, either call upon Archangels Michael and Chamuel or send the ghosts to the nearest morgue or funeral home. They can go into the light with others who are crossing over. More than one soul at a time can use the tunnel of light created for the newly departed.

These earthbound spirits feed off of our energy and target humans who have a similar fixation as their own: drug or alcohol abuse, emotional indulgences, trauma, or someone who is ungrounded and not fully participating in their own spiritual development. When the earthbound spirit finds an empath in a state of dissension, having weak or no boundaries, the earthbound spirit attaches itself to the victim's energy field. This is not a possession. I believe that only one soul can inhabit a body at a time, but a person with an entity attachment will feel out-of-sorts, be filled with dysfunctional thoughts, emotions, and have cravings that are not their own. The best way to keep these entities away is to raise your personal vibration, keep your aura close to your body, and remove negative or stuck energy so these beings are no longer attracted to you.

Mary Ann has seen and communicated with earthbound souls since she was four years old and is able to create the light and give earthbound souls a second chance to cross over. In her book, she gives several reasons why souls do not cross over immediately:

- They are attached to things such as jewelry, cars, houses, furniture, or places where they lived found comfort, or died

- They are busybodies who don't want to leave
- They are seeking revenge or pursuing justice
- They fear judgment or punishment on the other side
- They want to protect the living

Mary Ann Winkowski is the consultant for the creators of the CBS show, *The Ghost Whisperer,* in which Jennifer Love Hewitt stars. The first time I saw this show, I cried for joy because finally someone had an explanation as to why souls were coming to me. I sensed they wanted help, but I didn't know what to do for them. Even though I had sensed the presence of spirits all my life, I had no idea that I was a "ghost whisperer" (a.k.a. medium) as well as an empath. No wonder my life was so crazy while I was ignorant of these very important facts. Knowledge is power. As I learned to follow my own heart and develop spiritual intelligence, I began setting boundaries with these disembodied souls. I started calling upon angels, archangels, and my own spirit guides whenever a soul came to me for help. Archangels Michael and Chamuel can help these lost souls find a place of peace in the afterlife. At first, I visualized the soul leaving, but once I knew my effort was working, I relaxed and enjoyed my new-found privacy with the assurance that my "team" was taking care of things.

Now whenever I sense an entity, I immediately ask "who are you and what do you need?" If the spirit will not answer those two questions, they are not permitted to stay in my presence. For example, I was keeping my grandsons at their home while their parents were away for a week celebrating their tenth wedding anniversary.

Within a matter of hours of being the only adult in the house, I began sensing an ominous presence—especially whenever I was in the bedroom and or bathroom. It was eerie and I felt like I was being watched. The spirit was my daughter-in-law's father. Perhaps "sperm donor" is a more fitting term for him. Amanda never knew the man because he abandoned her family when she was about a year old. Since this was not my home and I didn't know if Amanda wanted her father around in order to resolve some issue she might have with him, I set a boundary that would not allow his spirit to come near me, my grandsons, or their property as long as I was there. I let Amanda know about this when she returned and she immediately decided to maintain the boundary.

There are times when a spirit has a personal message for me or another person. If I can deliver the message without causing discomfort to myself, I will try to do so. The day before Amanda and my son returned home, Amanda's mother, Kendra ("Nanna K" as her grandchildren called her), dropped by in spirit. I knew and loved Kendra and didn't even have to ask who the spirit was. There was a lightness, warmth, and sense of love surrounding me as I heard her say, "I'm just dropping by to check on my babies. It's good to see you here. Thank you for all you do for Amanda and the boys." I related this message to Amanda, who received the news with tears of joy. Those are the times when I am glad I can consciously interact with spirits.

Honor the Boundaries of Others

By being overly sympathetic toward others we enable them to continue their harmful behavior. This not only disempowers them, it adversely affects you. I hate to be so blunt, but we empaths really need to mind our own business. We have enough stuff of our own to deal with; we don't need someone else's drama. We are all here to enjoy our earth experience, explore possibilities, and develop our own soul. When we carry burdens for someone else, we rob them of the experience to learn specific lessons their soul has arranged.

If someone close has asked for some space or time apart from you, honor their request. We don't have to be entertained or always together in order to have a healthy relationship. If your partner needs space, you don't have to feel as though they don't like you or don't want to be with you. They may simply need a break from your energy—especially if you are carrying a negative charge and are not attempting to clear it. Give your loved one a chance to recover and recharge their batteries. Why not spend the time engaging in your own spiritual work? It can only make your relationship better.

You are stronger than you think you are. You are *not* a victim; you have the power to choose. Therefore, there is no need to blame others or circumstances for your discomfort. As you begin the process of working on your own stuff, you will see your "self" in a new light. You will see your life shift in miraculous ways and you will attract many new opportunities. And you won't be burdened with other people's stuff.

Detach

An empath's best coping method is the ability to detach from others or a situation. An empath is a feeler, but we know when we've reached our limit. If the emotional burden of another becomes too great, we can pull away without being hateful, angry, or upset with that person.

It is an essential act of self preservation that must be utilized.

I find that being in a crowd for a long period of time is still overwhelming for me, even though I have done everything I recommend in this book. So, for social gatherings where there will be a lot of unfamiliar energy, I either stay near someone I know or engage in conversation with someone whose energy feels good—I generally gravitate toward children! If I start to feel overwhelmed, I'll find a corner where I can observe the action without being antisocial or placing myself right in the middle of things. That allows me to take breaks without being missed while I go outside or to a quiet room to get away from the cacophony of energy. If my husband goes with me to a social event and I start feeling over stimulated, I can stand near him or hold his hand for a moment to help ground myself with his energy. If I do this several times, he knows I am ready to leave and will look for a way to politely say our goodbyes. If I am going to a function without my husband, I may drive my own car so I'm not stranded if I need to leave.

These days, if I pray for anyone, I do not allow myself to become emotionally involved. I no longer assume to know the plan for another person's soul. I refuse to usurp the free will of others as I did many times in my religious prayer efforts when I was trying to save the world. Instead, I send people divine love and light—a beneficial energy they can use however they need to. Since I am directing a higher energy rather than sending out my own energy, I am not taking on the detrimental energy my prayer recipients release from their blocked chakras, auras, or body cells. I am detached from the recipient's energy.

Non-resistance

Fear, judgment, denial, and our preconceived ideas about a person, place, or opportunity can mislead us, but those who have developed the gift of empathy and learned to trust their intuition are more inclined to pay attention to what they sense and feel. This allows energy to flow through without getting stuck, while at the same time being grounded and centered. This is what I refer to as being non-resistant.

In our society, we have been taught to be emotionally dishonest. We pretend to feel one thing when we truly feel another. When we are sad, we say everything is fine, yet a large percentage of people are taking antidepressants. When we are angry and our spouse asks, "What's wrong?" we pretend not to be upset. We say, "Nothing's the matter" or we give them the silent treatment rather than calmly and rationally expressing our point of view. When we deny what we feel or judge ourselves for feeling it, we deny an authentic part of ourselves. If we resist or ignore what is happening or what we feel, we can't process the experience. I'm not advocating a full-blown, violent expression of emotions. There is a healthy way to acknowledge our feelings without letting them get the best of us or harm others.

I was raised by parents who verbally fussed and fought with little regard for one another's feelings. Nothing ever seemed to be resolved from this activity. Being an energy sensitive individual, I hated this turmoil because I wanted to fix things. As a teenager, I would take sides and try to help them resolve their problems. That only made things worse. So, when I got married the first time (at age seventeen), I decided to not raise any opposition with my partner. No matter how much I didn't like what was going on in my marriage, I would have peace at all cost. You know how that turned out. I nearly died before I left that marriage twenty-two years later.

Even though I was healing as I released pent up emotions from my first marriage, I brought a lot of codependent behaviors into my second marriage. I continued to walk on eggshells to avoid an argument. I didn't realize it at the time, but I was accumulating new "stuff" and I released old energy. On the other hand, my new husband was one to just "let it rip" when it came to expressing his displeasure about anything. After ten years together, we are always authentic and truthful with one another, even when we are upset. Applying what we learned in *The Four Agreements* by Don Miguel Ruiz and *A Course in Miracles*, we learned to maturely resolve our conflicts in a win-win manner without holding grudges or stuffing our feelings. For the first few years of our marriage we had sticky notes posted throughout our house that reminded us to "be impeccable with your word, don't take anything personally, don't make assumptions, and always do your best." Rather than perceiving a disagreement as a personal attack, we either personally acknowledge whatever emotion we feel and then let it go without mentioning it to the other person, or we talk about what's upsetting us and resolve the issue together. This non-blaming, non-resistant method of dealing with life's troubles has transformed our relationship and given us freedom to feel what we feel, express our personal likes/dislikes, and be totally honest with ourselves and one another. As we are connected with life and with our own being, we find that emotional suffering is not needed.

Whatever we place emphasis on will increase.

Resistance attracts things, people, energy, and situations we don't want. Therefore, I'm more concerned with raising my vibration, enjoying my spiritual practice, and maintaining my own energy than I am with setting up fortresses to protect myself against external forces.

One of the most natural ways to make sure you are carrying only your own energy is to stop resisting, pushing away, or struggling for or against anything. When you move into the stream of life, things begin to fall into perfect alignment, synchronicities abound, aches and pains diminish, stress melts away, creativity flourishes, relationships heal, and we experience a profound sense of peace.

Julie Isaac shares her story about being non-resistant:

> *Years ago, when I was about to move in with my mother and take care of her, I had a choice to make. Since I've always picked up other people's energy (especially physical illnesses), I asked myself, "Do I take steps to protect myself from her energy, or not?"*
>
> *Because she was my mother, it didn't feel right to protect myself from her. So I didn't. I assumed that I would pick up her pain and problems, and I made peace with that happening. To my surprise, I discovered that the less I "protected" myself from her energy, the less I was affected by it. And it wasn't just because she was my mother. I discovered that this was true with everyone. The less I held an energetically defensive posture, the less I was affected by other people's energy. This may not be true for everyone, but it changed my life and how I am in the world.*

We resist because we are fearful or in denial. We resist our emotions because we are afraid to feel. Perhaps we are afraid our emotions will take over. Quite the opposite is true. Our emotions, when stuffed, are silently taking over our well-being. When we resist someone or something (even if it is unpleasant) rather than accept what is, it only makes things worse. Being resistant blinds us to possibilities and solutions and causes us to become stuck, defensive, shut down, and reactive. Our body may feel tight, tense, or lethargic; our emotions may feel heavy, sad, or angry. If something is upsetting you, deal with it quickly rather than denying its reality. That which resists, persists! If you notice you are in a state of resistance, go back to Chapter 9 and do some of the exercises that bring peace of mind, balance, and well-being.

Sources for Chapter 10:

1. Grey, Gini. "How Empaths Can Create Healthy Boundaries." 10 July 2010. Accessed 6 January 2011. <http://www.ginigrey.com/wp/spiritual-insights/energy-boundaries>.

Chapter 11 ~ How to Work with Empathic Energy

Most who read this book may be desperate to be free of the stuff they've already picked up and want to prevent further emotional overload. Therefore, the focus of this book is on clearing and protecting empaths from picking up the energy of others rather than on teaching empaths to become healers. However, since so many empaths are natural healers, I want to touch briefly on this topic in case some of you want to go a step farther and seek training that will help you use your empathic gift as a natural healer or psychic practitioner. You certainly don't have to take this path if you don't want to, but you may find it beneficial to learn to "read" the feelings of others without taking out their trash!

Let's begin by understanding the difference between intuition and empathy. I've used the words interchangeably throughout this book, but there is a distinction to be made. Intuition is the collective body of our internal guidance system, which goes far beyond common sense and includes (but is not limited to) telepathy, pre-cognizance, clairvoyance, clairaudience, clairsentience, and empathy. Empathy is one part of this divine guidance system. Being empathic allows us to pick up information with the five commonly accepted senses: sight, hearing, smell, feeling/touch, and taste to bring us a message about others. Empathy naturally wants to help others by easing their emotional burdens or carrying their pain for them. Empathy brings in information and energy (info-energy) like a radio picking up multiple channels all at once. The brain does not know what to do with all this random input. We must interpret the information we receive.

It is much wiser to get information about people through the broader scope of intuition by communicating directly with the over soul of those you want to help. Intuition is internal, unlike the environmental energy you have been picking up from those around you, and does not invade the field of another person in order to glean information. It is your own mind, divine self, or over soul speaking to you from a higher perspective—like a bird's-eye view—and assisting you in making good decisions and avoiding trouble. Coming from the universal mind where all knowledge is stored, this insight is direct, impartial, unemotional, and does not discriminate or judge. Unlike empathy, intuition does not demand attention or impose upon you or others. It sees the bigger picture and offers suggestions and information accordingly, but you have to decide what to do with it. There are times when you will hear your intuition telling you to avoid a situation or person. It might tell you to take a different route to work and later you find that an accident took place on your normal route about the time you would have arrived at that location. Unfortunately, most people are so busy, stressed out, frustrated, upset, or angry they don't take time to listen to the gentle and wise voice within. Thus, they miss important messages that could have eased their own burden.

How many times have you said or thought, "If I had only listened to myself, such and such would not have happened?" Your intuition is an aspect of divine guidance—our higher consciousness or spirit talking to us. By ignoring our intuition, situations do not generally turn out as well as they could have. For example, I needed more yarn to complete a crochet project. K-Mart is about two miles away and I was pretty certain I had seen yarn there. That little voice in my head told me I should call first to make sure they sell yarn or else go directly to the Wal-Mart, which is about five miles in the opposite direction. I was in a hurry so I went to the closer store first, only to find that they no longer sell yarn. I ended up wasting time and gas because I ignored my intuition. That was a minor inconvenience compared to what could have happened in 2005 when I was having problems with my bowels. I called my doctor, who did a non-invasive test that showed absolutely nothing out of the ordinary. He dismissed my condition, calling it chronic diarrhea. Not satisfied with his diagnosis, I listened to my body, followed my intuition, and sought a second opinion. This doctor performed a colonoscopy, which revealed polyps and a large tumor in my colon. Immediate surgery was planned and about eight inches of my colon was removed. Had I ignored my intuition that time, the tumor could have developed into a cancerous mass. By the way, the formation of the tumor was not a result of carrying anyone else's energy at that time. It was a cumulative detrimental effect from all the years I stuffed my true "gut" feelings. When it came up for healing I had to get rid of it.

There is a way to read the energy of others in a safe manner. Healers often empathically tune into their clients on a conscious level to be able to get in touch with symptoms and any prominent issues. By receiving information in this manner, healers intuitively diagnose and offer treatment, but they may also pick up on detrimental energy that must be cleared immediately after each session.

If you decide to read energy as a healer, make sure your own house is in order and that you are carrying only your own energy. Otherwise, it may be very difficult to separate your stuff from what belongs to the client. Before you begin, ground your energy and use your breath to center yourself in a calm emotional state. Visualize light filling your head and emanating out of your third eye (sixth chakra), located in the center of your forehead, to see what is going on in the mind, chakras, aura, and life of your client. Ask a question of the client's over soul or your own higher self, and allow a vision that represents the answer to appear in your mind. When using your third eye you will get a sense of knowing that does not have to register in your emotions or body. Share with the client what you sense, hear, or see. When you are done with the reading, let the energy used in the session flow out through your root chakra or through your feet and into the ground.

For more help on learning to use your intuition for healing, see the list of books in the resources at the back of this book.

Chapter 12 ~ The Next Step

Each of us is responsible for the situations we create, the people we choose to associate with, and the way we live our lives. As powerful spirit beings, we have control over our own energy, body, moods, perspective, and decisions. You can consciously choose to stop taking on other people's heavy emotions and the negativity generated in crowds and start producing positive energy and thoughts. What you have done in the past has not worked, but you now have the tools to attract positive energy, heal yourself, and create a better life.

Finding freedom from the detrimental thoughts, feelings, and energy around you requires you to be aware of what's going on with your own energy. The best way to do this is to get off "autopilot" and stop attracting energy by default. How? By regularly spending time in a spiritual effort to raise your vibration. Set aside time each day to ground yourself, get in touch with your own energy, and clear your field. Keep practicing the techniques in this book and try others as well. As you shift your thoughts, attitudes, and emotions in an upward direction, you will naturally start to attract wonderful circumstances into your life.

I realize what a challenge it can be to stay positive in the emotionally charged world in which we live. It will help if you prepare in advance when you must go into public settings or social gatherings. Surround yourself with love and light, ground your energy, and center yourself before you leave home. When you find yourself in stressful situations, take a break and find a quiet place where you can close your eyes, breathe consciously, let go of the external world, and tap into your true essence. Ask your divine guidance to transmute any detrimental energy into beneficial energy that can bless and help everyone find peace and joy within.

Whenever you feel heavy emotions, take action quickly! Acknowledge and release them before they take over and drag you down. That way, you can be non-resistant and present in every moment as you bring your attention and awareness to each thought, feeling, and activity as it is occurring. When something upsetting is occurring for you, there are three choices you can make:

1) Resist, deny, avoid, or ignore it (*not* recommended!)

2) Communicate, ask for what you need, and be willing to alter what you can about the situation. If another person involved will not cooperate with your peace-making efforts, cut ties with the offender or remove yourself from the unhealthy environment. Change jobs, relocate, or do whatever you need to bring about a better living/working condition or peace of mind. You do not have to complain, suffer, or play the role of a victim.

3) Accept the situation once you have done all you can to remedy it. This does not mean you are giving up or surrendering to something you abhor. It means you have released all the negative charge surrounding the situation and come to a place of peace that will allow

you to remain where you are without suffering, stuffing, or seething. This option is best employed when you are dealing with an uncontrollable situation such as the death of a loved one or the termination of any close relationship.

When you are non-resistant, you feel lighter and it's easier to be joyful and allow what you really want to flow into your life. Happiness comes from within and is not dependent upon external circumstances.

To live without resistance, you must completely forgive yourself and others of any perceived wrongdoings. Grievances hold us back from living in a state of total peace and well-being. When we judge or criticize others or refuse to forgive, we block the natural flow of energy in our body and aura. This causes us to attract more negativity. So, the next time you are about to judge or criticize, stop and accept yourself, the other person, and situation as it is. It doesn't mean you condone it. It means you are accepting its reality instead of denying or fighting it.

Let go of the need to change people. The only person you can change is yourself. If you find that certain people and situations are draining, get away from their influence. Look for new opportunities and relationships with uplifting and positive people that will support and nurture you on your spiritual path. When we focus on cultivating and integrating a peaceful mindset into our lives, the universe will guide us to the resources that support our goal of entering into the flow of who we really are. Undoubtedly, your intuition led you to this book. You know how to access your internal guidance.

We have an unseen energy field around us that many far-easterners have known about since ancient times. The fact that most of us can't see magnetic energy fields or chakras causes some people to believe that these energy centers do not exist. Being able to tap into one another person's mental and emotional fields is proof that we are connected by some multi-dimensional source. Regardless of our beliefs or background it is easy to see that we are more than just our body—we are spirit beings. Some of you may think that being spiritual means being religious or vice versa, but I can assure you that is not always the case. Looking back in history it is easy to see how our fears have limited our spiritual growth and the evolution of humanity. Many people have formulated their belief system from teachings someone else handed down to them.

I hope that after reading this book you are ready to accept that you are a spirit being having a human experience and that as such, you have gifts that are of value to you and others. Learn to use these gifts wisely to help the world move into a new reality where we are led by the heart and mind of Spirit rather than ego. Things may not change overnight; it's not easy to switch from feeling doomed and powerless to feeling peaceful and enthusiastic. Take it one day at a time; observe your emotions and see them as part of your guidance system or a mirror to let you see what you are attracting. Life is full of ups and downs, and what you give your attention to is your choice. It will help to focus on what's going right in your life. If you notice small changes within yourself, celebrate and acknowledge what is working for you. This is a new beginning.

Like you, I will continue to grow in my understanding of God's mind and reach new levels of enlightenment. I enjoy sharing what I learn. I invite you to visit my Web site http://WeAre1InSpirit.com and my blog http://WeAreOneInSpirit.com for uplifting videos, audios, books, poems, and spiritual information. There, you will find my weekly podcast, *We Are One in Spirit*, designed to bring understanding, unity, and respect among diverse spiritual communities everywhere. Each Thursday at 7 PM Central Time, a new program is uploaded.

You are limitless! Live from the essence of who you are: a joyful, divine, spiritual being. As a result, you will feel uplifted and energized as your sensitivities blossom. Do not restrict your life experience by having your mind overly focused on the material world. You have the tools and strategies to cope, feel safe, and allow your gift to blossom. Chaos is unnecessary and you don't have to participate any longer. You can choose freedom from the thoughts, feelings, and energy of those around now.

Resources

Books

27 Ways to Feng Shui Your Home by Tisha Morris. (ISBN-13: 978-1596525672).

40 Days to Personal Revolution: A Breakthrough Program to Radically Change Your Body and Awaken the Sacred Within Your Soul by Baron Baptiste (ISBN-13: 978-0743227834).

7 Mindsets to Master Self-Awareness by Elizabeth Diamond (ISBN-13: 978-1452046235). www.creatingintentions.com.

A Course in Miracles by Helen Schucman and Bill Thetford. (ISBN-13: 978-0976420064).

An A-Z Aromatherapy by Patricia Davis (ISBN-13: 978-0091906610).

Angel Numbers 101 by Doreen Virtue (ISBN-13: 978-1401920012).

Animal Speak by Ted Andrews (ISBN-13: 978-0875420288).

Awakened Wisdom by Patrick Ryan (ISBN-10: 0984236309).

Celebration of Breath: Rebirthing, Book II; Or How to Survive Anything and Heal Your Body by Sondra Ray (ISBN-13: 978-0890873557).

CHAKRA POWER! How to Fire Up Your Energy Centers to Live a Fuller Life by Harriette Knight. (ISBN-13: 978-0982242704).

Complete Aromatherapy Handbook Essential Oils for

Radiant Health by Susanne Fischer-Rizzi. (ISBN-13: 978-0806982229).

Confessions of a Feng Shui Ghost-Buster by Anna Maria Prezio (ISBN-13: 978-1435706408). http://www.fengshuiharmony.net.

Conscious Breathing: Breathwork for Health, Stress Release, and Personal Mastery by Gay Hendrick (ISBN-13: 978-0553374438).

Emotional Freedom: Liberate Yourself From Negative Emotions and Transform Your Life (Harmony Books, 2009) by Judith Orloff. (ISBN-13: 978-0307338181. Her other bestsellers are *Positive Energy, Intuitive Healing,* and *Second Sight.* See www.drjudithorloff.com.

Flower Essence Repertory: A Comprehensive Guide to North American and English Flower Essences for Emotional and Spiritual Well-Being by Patricia Kaminski and Richard Katz (Jun 1994). (ISBN-13: 978-0963130617).

From Chaos to Calm: How to Shift Unhealthy Stress Patterns and Create Your Ideal Balance in Life by Gini Grey (ISBN-13: 978-1425929336).

Handbook of Moral Development by Melanie Killen. (ISBN-13: 978-0805861723).

Healing Herbs by Frank J. Lipp (ISBN-13: 978-0760781630).

Intuitive Connections, A Five Step Process to Embrace Your Intuition by Sandra Couts. An e-book available at http://embraceyourintuition.com. To obtain a hard copy, email coutssd@hotmail.com.

Kids Who See Ghosts, Guide Them Through Their Fear by Dr. Caron Goode (ISBN-13: 978-1578634729).

Memory in the Cells: How to change behavioral patterns and release the pain body by Luis Angel Diaz (ISBN-13: 978-0595523788).

Mirroring People: The Science of Empathy and How We Connect with Others by Marco Iacoboni Picador. (ISBN-13: 978-0312428389).

Moving Toward Balance: 8 Weeks of Yoga with Rodney Yee (ISBN-13: 978-0875969213).

Rebirthing in the New Age by Leonard Orr (ISBN-13: 978-1425114169).

Roots of Empathy: Changing the World Child by Child Mary Gordon (ISBN-13:978-1615190072).

Seasons of Aromatherapy, Hundreds of Recipes and Sensory Suggestions by Judith Fitzsimmons (ISBN-13: 978-1573241441).

Teaching Empathy: A Blueprint for Caring, Comp. by David A. Levine (ISBN-13: 978-1935249009).

The Age of Empathy: Nature's Lessons for a Kinder Society by Frans de Waal (ISBN-13: 978-0307407771).

The Astonishing Power of Emotions: Let Your Feelings Be Your Guide by Esther and Jerry Hicks (ISBN-13: 978-1401912468).

The Compassionate Instinct: The Science of Human Goodness by Dacher Keltner (ISBN-13: 978-0393337280).

The Empathic Civilization: The Race to Global Consciousness in a World in Crisis by Jeremy Rifkin (ISBN-10: 1585427659).

The Four Agreements by Don Miguel Ruiz (ISBN-13: 978-1878424501).

The Highly Sensitive Person by Elaine N. Aron, Ph.D. (ISBN-13: 978-0767903363).

The Pleiadian Workbook by Amora Quan Yin (ISBN-13: 978-1879181311).

The Sid Series ~ A Collection of Holistic Stories for Children by Yvonne Perry teaches children to honor their intuition and spiritual gifts. (ISBN-13: 978-0982572207).

The Social Neuroscience of Empathy by Jean Decety and William Ickes (ISBN-13: 978-0262515993).

The Spointaneous Healing of Belief, Shattering the Paradigm of False Limits (ISBN: 978-1401916909) by Gregg Braden.

When Ghosts Speak by Mary Ann Winkowski (ISBN-13: 978-0446581332).

Writing Down Your Soul: How to Activate and Listen to the Extraordinary Voice Within by Janet Conner (ISBN-13: 978-1573243568).

Yoga, Power, and Spirit by Alberto Villaldo (ISBN-13: 978-1401910471).

Dr. Rita Louise has three books of interest to empaths: *Dark Angels: An Insiders Guide to Ghosts, Spirits and Attached Entities, Avoiding The Cosmic 2X4*, and The Power Within. See http://www.soulhealer.com for details.

Classes and Groups

Elise Lebeau has information on her Web site for empaths: http://www.eliselebeau.com/empaths. She also sponsors a networking group for empathic people to connect and find community at http://empathcommunity.eliselebeau.com.

Online courses by Harriette Knight are offered on an ability-to-pay basis at www.DailyOm.com. Choose from How to Fire Up Your Chakras, A Year of Intuitive Illuminations, and The Power of Gemstones.

The School of Empath Psychology offers free online lessons for developing the gift of empathy. See the curriculum at http://mysilentecho.com. There is an online Yahoo group http://groups.yahoo.com/group/Empaths/ that serves as a discussion forum for students of the school for empaths.

Practitioners

Dr. Caron B. Goode, ED.D., NCC, DAPA is a parenting-training coach (http://coachingparents.wordpress.com and www.HeartWiseParent.com) with a focus on spiritual relationships, wellness, women's psychology, and health. She is the author of *The Art & Science of Coaching Parents; Raising Intuitive Children* (2009 Best Parenting Book in US News Awards); and *Kids Who See Ghosts - Guide Them Through Their Fears.* Visit www.AcademyforCoachingParents.com to learn about training to become a parent coach. Phone her at 817-847-8758.

Cherise Thorne, the founder of New Dawn Ascension, offers intuitive insight into areas of life or body that may be blocked. http://www.newdawnascension.com. The Enlightened Living program is part of the Seminary Teacher Training Program Cherise and her mother, Angela, present online at http://www.knowingspirit.org.

Denise Demaras (www.denisedemaras.com) has an on-line source of information, support, and techniques for healing holistically. www.holistichealingpractices.com

Donna Seebo is a medium, radio show host, and an empath. As an author, publisher, lecturer and renowned mental practitioner and counselor, Donna offers private consultations in person or by telephone: (800) 872-8852. Learn more at http://delphiinternational.com.

Harriette Knight is a master healer and psychic-medium, who conducts re-connective healing sessions in person or distantly. Psychic messages are recorded on CD. To schedule an appointment, call 661-254-4747 or visit http://www.harrietteknight.com.

Ranoli is able to clear a home of detrimental energy and set the stage for bringing in beneficial energy. Contact her at PO Box 1267 Littleton, CO 80160. (303) 797-0884 http://www.heartandhomehealing.com.

Gini Grey is a transformational coach who reads energy and teaches others to do the same. By learning to create healthy energy boundaries, differentiating her energy from others' energy, and clearing her field, she was able to start reading energy using clairvoyance instead of feeling energy through clairsentience. Find her online at www.ginigrey.com or www.ginigrey.com/spiritualtransformers.

Rita Louise, PhD, offers intuitive counseling, energy medicine, nutritional counseling. See http://www.soulhealer.com/contact.htm

Sally Hinkle is an intuitive energy consultant whose practice also encompasses pet health and environmental balance. Her studies and certifications include the following spiritually-guided healing and energy balancing modalities: Reiki, Vortex Alignment, Life Alignment, Body Spin, and Transference Healing. www.SallyHinkle.com

Sandra Couts is an intuitive counselor, workshop facilitator, and certified Healing Touch practitioner. She is also a twin whose empathic connection to her twin was a gift and a challenge. She is the author of *Intuitive Connections, A Five Step Process to Embrace Your Intuition.* Her email is coutssd@hotmail.com or you may visit her online at http://sandracouts.com or http://embraceyourintuition.com.

Tisha Morris, the author *of 27 Ways to Feng Shui Your Home,* is a feng shui consultant for home or office. Located in the Nashville area, she also works remotely to help you create harmony in your environment. See http://www.tishamorris.com.

Author and counselor, Dr. Tom Goode is an insightful and engaging speaker with more than thirty years of spiritual experience to share. He is available for workshops, retreats, lectures, interviews and presentations on topics that include, but are not limited to, holistic health and healing, spirituality, higher consciousness, transcendence, and transformational psychology. For more information see www.DrTomGoode.com or call 817-847-8216. You may contact him through his Web site: http://internationalbreathinstitute.com/contact.

Quizzes and Tests

Are You Emotionally Free? Take The Emotional Freedom Test 20 Questions for Reflection http://www.drjudithorloff.com/free-articles.htm

Take the quiz at

http://quizfarm.com/quizzes/quiz/EmberDust/what-empathic-type-are-you to learn what type of empath you are.

Take this quiz to see if you are a natural born empath. http://healing.about.com/library/quiz/hsp/blhspquiz.htm.

Test to see how open or active are your chakras at http://www.eclecticenergies.com/chakras/chakratest.php.

Radio Shows

Donna Seebo is a radio show host and empath. *The Donna Seebo Show* airs 3-4 p.m. Pacific Time, Monday through Friday. Callers are welcome to call the worldwide toll-free number (888) 815-9756 during air time. All broadcasts are archived so you can listen to broadcasts any time. http://www.bbsradio.com/bbc/donna_seebo.php

Faith Ranoli's *Heal your home - transform your life! Radio Show* airs each week at http://www.healthylife.net. Faith Ranoli PO Box 1267 Littleton, CO 80160. Phone (303) 797-0884.

Harriette Knight's Psychic & Healing Hour airs each Wednesday on BlogTalkRadio (http://www.blogtalkradio.com/harrietteknight) at 6 p.m. She gives free psychic readings on her radio show.

Katheryn Tidwell Bieber and Elizabeth Diamond have an Internet radio show known as *Awakening the HeART of Your Creative Soul*. It airs at 10 p.m. EST on Blog Talk Radio. http://www.blogtalkradio.com/awakeningtheheartofyourcreativesoul.

The Hillary Raimo Show airs Thursdays at 8 p.m. EST on Achieve Radio. She also offers healing sessions, UNtrainings, and metaphysical trips. See www.hillaryraimo.com

Dr. Rita Louise, PhD, ND is the host of *Just Energy Radio*. (http://www.justenergyradio.com/) On each show, she provides guidance and advice on physical, emotional, work, and relationship problems.

We Are One in Spirit discusses spiritual topics such as healing, metaphysics, energy modalities, ghosts, afterlife, near-death, and other spiritually transforming experiences. See http://weareoneinspirit.com

Jewelry

Amanda McCurley's gemstone jewelry shop http://www.etsy.com/shop/eidolajewelry.

Harriette Knight's Charity Clarity jewelry http://www.charityclarityjewelry.com

Vidcos, CDs, DVDs

bj King's *Affirmation for Cellular Release of Fear* releases deep trauma, negative energy, and judgments at the cellular level in order to end destructive behavior patterns and free you from negativity. To order, call 405-773-5210 or write to her at PO Box 22174, Oklahoma City, OK 73123. Her email is Namastebj@cox.net.

Free mini video classes on Youtube: *Dr. Orloff's Living Room Series* to learn about the special method Dr. Orloff recommends to remember your dreams and other topics to build the power within www.youtube.com/judithorloffmd.

Getting into the Vortex by Esther and Jerry Hicks contains four powerfully guided daily meditations that have been designed to get you into the Vortex of Creation in four basic areas of your life: General Well-Being, Financial Well-Being, Physical Well-Being, and Relationships. http://ow.ly/3c2ye

http://www.gaiam.com/category/yoga-studio.do is a great store for DVDs, clothing, mats, props, and other products related to yoga.

Rodney Yee's *Yoga for Beginners* (ASIN: B001F76OKC).

Steven Halpern's *Chakra Suite* (ASIN: B000050MHN) is one of the first CDs I bought to help clear my chakras. Published by Inner Peace Music in 2001, it is still one of my favorites. http://www.innerpeacemusic.com

Terry Oldfield's *Chakra Clearing Meditation* published by New Earth in 2009 (ASIN: B0023X26UO) is available as an audio CD or MP3 download on Amazon.com.

Thea Surasu's *Singing Bowls of Shangri-la* published by Inner Peace Music in 1998 (ASIN: B00000DC1R) is available at http://www.innerpeacemusic.com or on Amazon.com

Tom Goode demonstrates full wave breathing on a video series at http://wn.com/Full_Wave_Breathing_with_Doctor_Tom_Goode. You may read Tom's articles on breathwork at http://internationalbreathinstitute.com/category/blog.

Twenty Gems, Journey to the Self (http://www.twentygems.net) by Denna Shelton are

Resources

DVDs and digital downloads that can be played at work, on a laptop computer, and on your iPhone or iPad. The beautiful nature scenery, mesmerizing animations, soothing music, and positive affirmations combine to give a refreshing lift to your spirit.

Bibliography

"Being Empathic Comes from the Heart." AskGrace.com. Accessed 18 November 2010. <http://www.askgrace.com/psychic_advice/0641_being_em path.htm>.

"Empathy: big feelings from little ones." Talaris Research Institute on Raising Children Network. Accessed 18 November 2010. <http://ow.ly/3cN1M>.

"Galileo Galilei." Wikipedia.com. Accessed 21 November 2010. <http://en.wikipedia.org/wiki/Galileo_Galilei>.

Alexander, Jadoa Tai. "Empathy 101." The Book of Storms Lessons in Dreamtongue. "Accessed 18 November 2010. <http://mysilentecho.com/dreamtongue1.htm>

Alexander, Jadoa Tai. The Book of Storms Stage 5. "Connecting to Your Inner Empath." <http://mysilentecho.com/lesson5.html >. Accessed 18 November 2010.

Andrews, Ted. Animal Speak. Llewellyn Publications, Woodbury, Minnesota, 2009. Pgs. 121-122, 124-125.

Bailey, Alice. "The Great Invocation." Accessed 18 November 2010. <http://www.lucistrust.org/>.

Beyerl, Paul. The Master Book of Herbalism. Phoenix Publishing, 1984.

Braden, Gregg. The Spontaneous Healing of Belief, Shattering the Paradigm of False Limits. Hay House, 2008. P 65.

Brant, Martha and Pat Winger. "Reading Your Baby's Mind." Newsweek society section (PDF). August 2005. Accessed 18 November 2010. <http://ow.ly/30W9w >.

Clark, Arthur, J. "Empathy: an integral model in the counseling process (Practice & Theory)." Journal of Counseling and Development. June 22, 2010.

Cline, Austin. "Pope John Paul II, Darwin, and Evolution." Catholic Opinions on Evolutionary Origins. About.com.

Accessed 20 November 2010.
<http://atheism.about.com/od/popejohnpaulii/a/evolution.
htm>.

Davis, Patricia. An A-Z Aromatherapy. The C.W. Daniel Company
Ltd; Revised edition November 25, 2004.

Decety, J., & Meyer, M. (2008). From emotion resonance to
empathic understanding: A social developmental
neuroscience account Development and Psychopathology, 20
(04) DOI: 10.1017/S0954579408000503

Desmarquet, Michel. "How to see and Read the Aura: Part 3,"
Thiaoouba Prophecy. Accessed 18 November 2010.
<http://www.thiaoouba.com/see_aura_color.htm>.

Desy, Phylameana lila. "Flower Essence Remedies for Empaths."
Empath Remedies, About.com Guide. Accessed 1 November
2010. <http://healing.about.com/od/empathic/a/empath-
essences.htm..

Diaz, Luis Angel. Memory in the Cells. iUniverse. 2010. Page 14.

Fischer Rizzi, Susanne. Complete Aromatherapy Handbook
Essential Oils for Radiant Health. Sterling Publishing
Company, 1991.

Fitzsimmons, Judith. Seasons of Aromatherapy, Hundreds of
Recipes and Sensory Suggestions. Conari Press.

Grey, Gini. "Aura and Energy Boundaries." Insights & Inspiration.
30 June, 2009. Accessed 6 January 2011.
<http://www.ginigrey.com/wp/spiritual-insights/energy-
boundaries>.

Grey, Gini. "Healing Emotional Pain with Radical Acceptance."
Quips and Tips for Spiritual Seekers. 8 May 2010. Accessed 11
January 2011.
<http://theadventurouswriter.com/quipstipsspiritualseekers
/healing-emotional-pain-with-radical-acceptance>.

Grey, Gini. "How Empaths Can Create Healthy Boundaries." 10
July 2010. Accessed 6 January 2011. The Adventurous Writer.
<http://theadventurouswriter.com/quipstipsspiritualseekers
/how-empaths-can-create-healthy-boundaries/>.

Grey, Gini. "Staying Grounded." Insights & Inspiration. 14 May,
2009. Accessed 6 January 2011.

<http://www.ginigrey.com/wp/spiritual-insights/staying-grounded>.

Grey, Gini. Telephone interview. 7 July, 2010.

Isaac, Julie. Personal interview. 6 July, 2010.

Killen, Melanie. Handbook of Moral Development. Lawrence Erlbaum Associates, 2006.

King, bj. "Overcoming Unconscious Empathic Tendencies." Intentional Telepathic Communications with Your OverSoul. About.com Guide. Accessed 23 November 2010. <http://healing.about.com/cs/empathic/a/bjking_empath.ht m>.

Kirsch I, Deacon BJ, Huedo-Medina TB, Scoboria A, Moore TJ, et al. 2008 Initial Severity and Antidepressant Benefits: A Meta-Analysis of Data Submitted to the Food and Drug Administration. PLoS Med 5(2): e45. doi:10.1371/journal.pmed.0050045

Klinsky, Leslee J. "What is Entity Contamination?" Psychic Protection 101. Accessed 18 November 2010. <http://healing.about.com/od/empathic/a/psychicprotect.ht m>.

Lebeau, Elise. "Empath Ethics." Accessed 18 November 2010. <http://www.eliselebeau.com/bonus2.php>.

Lebeau, Elise. "Grounding Techniques." Accessed 24 November 2010. <http://www.eliselebeau.com/bonus1.php >.

New International Version of the Holy Bible. Zondervan, 1985.

Orloff, Dr. Judith. "How To Stop Absorbing Other People's Negative Emotions" Adapted from Emotional Freedom: Liberate Yourself From Negative Emotions and Transform Your Life. Harmony Books, 2009. Accessed 21 November 2010. <http://www.drjudithorloff.com/Free-Articles/how-to-stop-absorbing.htm>.

Orloff, Dr. Judith. Emotional Freedom: Liberate Yourself From Negative Emotions and Transform Your Life. Crown Archetype, 2009.

Rizzolatti, G., & Craighero, L. (2004). The Mirror-Neuron System. Annual Review of Neuroscience, 27 (1), 169-192 DOI:

10.1146/annurev.neuro.27.070203.144230.

Salovey, Peter and John D. Mayer. <u>Emotional Intelligence</u>. Dude Publishing, 2004.

Schucman, Helen. A Course in Miracles, Combined Volume: Text, Workbook for Students, Manual for Teachers, 2nd Edition. Foundation for Inner Peace, 1992.

Wells, Pamela. Goddess <u>WisdomTitles app for iPhone</u>. "Emperor." p 32. Artmagic Publishing, 2009. <http://www.wisdomtitles.com>.

Winkowski, Mary Ann. When <u>Ghosts Speak</u>. Grand Central Publishing, 2009.

About the Author

After recovering from years of religious addiction and an abusive relationship with church leaders, Yvonne M. Perry (also known as LavendarRose) is finally free to be recognized as one who operates in both worlds—that of spirit and physical reality. Living life to the fullest in Nashville, Tennessee, she is the author of twelve books, a freelance ghostwriter, podcast host, blogger, publisher, and the owner of Writers in the Sky Creative Writing Services (http://writersinthesky.com).

For the first forty years of her deeply southern life, Yvonne was enmeshed with the fundamental dogma of religion and lived according to the interpretation of the Bible that her family, society, and church leaders passed down to her. Before she had a label to put on her empathetic ability, the Georgia native called herself an intercessor carrying the burdens of others to the throne of grace. While praying for others she empathically took on their suffering until it severely challenged her emotional and physical health.

Realizing how much of her time and energy had been given to religious activities, she became angry at the church for not accepting her prophetic gifts. During a dark night of the soul, things suddenly changed when Yvonne's original soul left her body and a new soul walked in during a soul exchange (a pre-incarnation agreement). The new soul (LavendarRose) began releasing the karma and healing the emotional issues of the first soul. Embracing a totally different path and belief system, she now openly uses the psychic gifts the first soul brought in. Yvonne has accepted the call to operate in the mind of God, worship the Divine Mother, and ascend with the help of the ascended master, Jesus.

She is a graduate of American Institute of Holistic Theology where she earned a Bachelor of Science in Metaphysics. Her style of writing is lovingly controversial and challenges people's belief systems in order to help them move past what she calls "Sunday School mentality." She is the host of We Are One in Spirit Podcast, a talk show that offers people a chance to share spiritual insight and join cross-cultural hands.

During her five-year involvement with Toastmasters International, Yvonne earned the recognition of Distinguished Toastmaster, an award for exemplary speaking skills. She attained every level of accomplishment the organization offered as well as many awards in speaking competitions. A polished, metaphysical speaker, she is available to share her knowledge on a wide variety of spiritual topics such as walk-in/soul exchange, psychic gifts, empathy, ascension rituals, ghosts, afterlife, and near-death or other spiritually-transforming experiences. In her lectures, workshops, and discussion group forums she presents her spiritual gifts of compassion to those who are ready to let go of fear and fully embrace Divine love. Those who are coming out of traditional religions and seeking their own personal truth will appreciate her fresh interpretation of the Bible as it refers to oneness with God and ascending as Jesus did. Her teachings fit in well at Unity churches, new age workshops, and Earth-based spiritual gatherings.

Books by Yvonne Perry

Bliss in Divine Oneness, an audio book free to those who join We Are One in Spirit blog community (http://WeAreOneInSpirit.blogspot.com).

Email Episodes ~ A Hilariously Honest Look at Life (ISBN 978-0975387009).

More Than Meets the Eye about Death, Dying and Afterlife (ISBN-13: 978-0975387061) http://deathdyingafterlife.blogspot.com

My Mother's Bipolar, So What am I? co-authored with Angela Grett (ISBN-13: 978-1419620065).

Right to Recover ~ Winning the Political and Religious Wars Over Stem Cell Research in America (ISBN-13: 978-1933449418) http://right2recover.blogspot.com.

Stockpiled Poetry Introspective Thoughts About Life, God, and Other Things That Cannot Be Explained (ISBN-13: 978-0982572238) https://www.createspace.com/3493393

The Sid Series ~ A Collection of Holistic Stories for Children (ISBN-13: 978-0982572207) http://thesidseries.com.

The Sid Series Coloring Book (ISBN-13: 978-0982572214)